The International Schools Journal Compendium

Volume IV

The International Baccalaureate: pioneering in education

Dr Ian Hill, Deputy Director General of the IB

Editor
Dr Mary Hayden

John Catt Educational Ltd
2010

Published 2010 by John Catt Educational Ltd
12 Deben Mill Business Centre, Woodbridge IP12 1BL, UK
T: +44 (0)1394 389850 F: +44 (0)1394 386893
W: www.johncatt.com E: enquiries@johncatt.com

A CIP catalogue record for this book is available from the British Library.

ISBN: 978 1 904724 93 3

Designed and typeset by John Catt Educational Limited,
12 Deben Mill Business Centre, Woodbridge IP12 1BL, UK

Printed and bound in Great Britain by Bell and Bain Ltd, Glasgow, Scotland.

Contents

Glossary

NB – in 2008 the IB dropped the 'O' from their acronym – IBO became IB. This style has been used throughout.

AP	Advanced Placement Program
ARDAC	Assessment Research and Development Advisory Committee
CAS	Creativity, Action, Service
CASS	Creative and Aesthetic activity and Social Service
CEEB	College Entrance Examination Board
CEIC	Centre for the study of Education in an International Context
CEO	Chief Executive Officer
CERN	European Nuclear Research Centre
CIS	Conference of Internationally-minded Schools
CSV	Community Service Volunteers
ECIS	European Council of International Schools
ETA	European Teachers Association
GAC	Government Advisory Committee
GCE	General Certificate of Education
HL	Higher level
HRC	Heads Representative Committee
HSA	Heads Standing Association
HSC	Heads Standing Conference
IB	International Baccalaureate
IBAEM	IB Africa, Europe, Middle East
IBAP	IB Asia Pacific
IBE	International Bureau of Education
IBEX	IB Examinations office
IBLA	IB Latin America
IBNA	IB North America
ICT	Information and Communications Technology
IHRC	International Heads Representative Committee
ISA	International Schools Association
ISES	International Schools Examination Syndicate
ISS	International Schools Services
MYP	Middle Years Programme
NGO	Non-governmental organisation
OECD	Organisation for Economic Co-operation and Development
PNEU	Parents National Education Union

5

PYP	Primary Years Programme
RHRC	Regional Heads Representative Committee
SAT	Scholastic Aptitude Test
SCG	Standing Conference of Governments
SL	Standard level (previously subsidiary level)
SNCF	*Société des Chemins de Fer Français*
ToK	Theory of Knowledge
UN	United Nations
UNESCO	United Nations Educational, Scientific and Cultural Organisation
UNICEF	United Nations Children's Fund
UNIS	United Nations International School
UWC	United World College
VSO	Voluntary Service Overseas
WHO	World Health Organisation

Biographies

Dr Ian Hill has been Deputy Director General of the International Baccalaureate (IB) Organization, based in Geneva, from 2000 to the present. Prior to joining the IB in 1993 as regional director for Africa, Europe and the Middle East, he was director of the International School of Sophia Antipolis, a bilingual IB diploma school near Nice, France. From 1986 to 1989 he was senior private secretary/advisor to the Minister for Education in the state of Tasmania and represented Australian government ministers of education on the IB Council of Foundation in Geneva. In Australia he held positions as teacher and deputy head in government schools while lecturing part-time in university teacher education. He has published numerous papers and book chapters on international education and co-authored with Jay Mathews of the *Washington Post* newspaper *Supertest: how the International Baccalaureate can strengthen our schools* (Open Court, Illinois, 2005).

His PhD thesis *The International Baccalaureate: policy process in education* is the source of much of the content of his writings about the history of the IB. He has been a member of the editorial advisory board for the *Journal of Research in International Education*, from the inception of the journal in 2002.

Dr Mary Hayden is Director of the Centre for the study of Education in an International Context (CEIC) at the University of Bath. Her postgraduate teaching and research supervision of Masters and Doctoral students worldwide focus particularly on international schools and international education, an area in which she has published widely. Prior to taking up her appointment with the University of Bath she worked in the research department at the University of London Examinations and Assessment Council and, for nine years, for the International Baccalaureate. More recently she edited *IB World* magazine for a one year period. She is currently a member of the International Primary Curriculum (IPC) Advisory Board, academic advisor to the International Leadership Management Programme (ILMP), editor of the *Journal of Research in International Education*, and a founding Trustee of the Alliance for International Education.

Ian Hill's published works on international education

As well as the articles published in this compendium, which originally appeared in the *International Schools Journal* (see contents for the full references for each article), Dr Hill has the following international publications to his name:

Journal articles

The international baccalaureate for Australia? (co-author) *Institute of Public Affairs Education Policy Unit Study Paper,* No 15, Aug 1989, pp1-14. (Reprinted in *Education Monitor,* Vol 1, No2, Spring 1989, pp17-20.)

The international baccalaureate and Australia, in the *Australian College of Education Tasmanian Chapter Newsletter,* No 79, Nov 1989, pp4-10.

IB developments in Australia, in *International Schools Journal,* No 19, Spring 1990, pp26-34.

The international baccalaureate: what contribution to Australian education? in *Unicorn (Journal of the Australian College of Education),* Vol 16, No 4, Nov 1990, pp234-235.

Le baccalauréat international: son histoire et sa contribution à l'enseignement interculturel, in *Savoir – Education Formation* (Ministère de l'Education Nationale – Paris), No 4, décembre 1995, pp617-632.

The international baccalaureate: an international model of curriculum and assessment development, in *Context – Magazine Européen de l'Education,* No 9, 1995.

Le baccalauréat international – passeport européen et mondial pour accéder aux études supérieures, in *Context – Magazine Européen de l'Education,* No 13, 1996.

IB Acceptance: No Two Universities Think Alike, in *IB World,* 1996, pp22-24.

The Spirit Finds Wings in Africa, in *IB World,* 1998, pp12-15.

Health Education in Practice, in *IB World,* 1999, p11.

Reflections on a Chinese Past/SOUL Project, in *IB World,* 1999, p27.

Internationally-minded schools, in *International Schools Journal,* Vol XX, No 1, November 2000, pp24-37.

Curriculum development and ethics in international education/Les programmes d'éducation internationale et la question éthique, in *Disarmament Forum,* No 3, 2001, pp49-58. UNIDR (United Nations Institute for Disarmament Research), Geneva. Available in English and French on the following website: www.unog.ch/UNIDIR/

Response to Gautam Sen's Article: 1, in *IB Research Notes 1*, No 3, 2001, p10. Community Service and Insight, in *IB World*, August 2001, No 28, pp8-9.

The International Baccalaureate: policy process in education, in *Journal of Research in International Education*, Vol 1, No 2, December 2002, pp 183-211.

IBO partnerships: influencing the quality of international education, in *International Schools Journal*, Vol XXIV, No 2, April 2005, pp32-39.

The arts and IB programmes, in *Scene (Quarterly Journal of the International Schools Theatre Association)*, December 2005, issue 2, pp6-7.

Do International Baccalaureate programs internationalise or globalise? in *International Education Journal*, Vol 7, No 1, March 2006, pp98-108. http://iej.cjb.net

Student types, school types, and their combined influence on the development of intercultural understanding, in *Journal of Research in International Education*, Vol 5, No 1, April 2006, pp 5-33.

Multicultural and international education: never the twain shall meet? in *International Review of Education*, Vol 53, No 3, May 2007, pp245-264.

Bac to the future: the international baccalaureate, in *Edge*, Vol 3, No 3, January/February 2008. Phi Delta Kappa International: Bloomington, Indiana, USA, pp1-18.

How IB Prepares Students for the World, in *Educational Leadership* (ASCD - Association for Supervision and Curriculum Development), May 2008, pp1-4. (co-authored with Jeffrey Beard)

Historical vignettes: John Goormaghtigh, in *International Schools Journal*, Vol XXVIII, No 1, November 2008, pp82-86.

Historical vignettes: Gérard Renaud, in *International Schools Journal*, Vol XXVIII, No 2, April 2009, pp87-92.

Historical vignettes: Ruth Bonner IB pioneer, in *International Schools Journal*, Vol XXIX, No 2, April 2010, pp82-86.

Book reviews

Diane Ravitch, *Left Back: A century of battles over School Reform*. NY: Simon & Schuster, 2000, in the *Journal of Research in International Education*, Vol 2, No 2, August 2003, pp240-243.

Book

Co-author with Jay Mathews, *Supertest: how the International Baccalaureate can strengthen our schools*. Open Court, Illinois. 2005.

Chapters in books

Do you want an international education? in *The International Herald Tribune: the executive's guide to international schools*. Kogan Page: London 2000, ppix -xiv.

The history of international education: an International Baccalaureate perspective, in Hayden, M., Thompson, J., Walker, G., (eds), *International Education in Practice: dimensions for national & international schools*. Kogan Page, London, 2002, pp18-29.

The International Baccalaureate, in Phillips, G., & Pound, T., (eds), *The Baccalaureate: A model for curriculum reform*, Kogan Page, London, 2003, pp47-76.

Phenomenal growth of the IB (pp239-280); The people who made the IBO (pp281-300); Looking ahead (pp301-321), in Peterson, A., *Schools Across Frontiers: Second Edition*, Open Court, Illinois, 2003.

International baccalaureate programmes and educational reform, in Hughes, P., (ed), *Secondary Education at the Crossroads*, Springer, Dordrecht, The Netherlands, 2006, pp15-68. (Phillip Hughes is Emeritus Professor at the Centre for UNESCO, Australian National University (Canberra).)

International education as developed by the International Baccalaureate Organization, in Hayden, M., Levy, J., and Thompson, J., (eds), *Sage Handbook of research in international education*, Sage: London, 2006, pp25-37.

A pedagogy for international education, in MacLean, R., (ed), *Learning and teaching for the twenty-first century,* Springer (The Netherlands), 2007, pp35-55.

Awaiting publication

Influencing mainstream systems of education, in Walker, G., (ed), *The changing face of international education,* IB Publishing, 2011.

An international model of world class education: the IB, in *Prospects,* 2011.

Introduction

Anyone joining a school that offers one or more of the International Baccalaureate Programmes (Primary Years Programme, Middle Years Programme and Diploma Programme) could be forgiven for not being concerned about the earlier days of the IB organisation and how it got to be where it is today. Few of us, in our day-to-day dealings with a range of organisations, will give much thought to how they came into being. Those who do take the time to read the various chapters in this compendium, however, will find a fascinating account of how the IB came to be the influential player it currently is. Not least among the aspects that give pause for thought are the fact that the original impetus for the organisation came from a small number of teachers in different parts of the world who recognised the need for a curriculum that prepared young people for a future not simply constrained by national boundaries – physical and cultural – and who were prepared to put energy, enthusiasm and huge amounts of time into achieving that end. The story of how their good idea, energy and enthusiasm, coupled with courage and determination, translated into securing support and funding from influential individuals and organisations – and then snowballed into having offices, paid members of staff and, eventually, three programmes that are offered not only in international schools but also in state-funded schools worldwide – reminds us of the salience of Margaret Mead's advice that we 'Never doubt that a small group of thoughtful, committed people can change the world.'

Who would have thought in the 1960s that this good idea would have led, some 40 years on, to a situation where over 3000 schools located in some 140 countries offer one or more of three IB programmes? Who would have imagined that the notion of an international curriculum as desirable would have translated into something of a necessity, with the IB laying the foundations for the development of a number of other international programmes offered in a rapidly growing number of schools? In many respects the earliest proponents of what became the IB were visionaries, ahead of their time. Before the concept of globalisation entered our collective consciousness, they sowed the seeds of a form of education encouraging young people to be internationally-minded, to think beyond their home context, to feel responsibility for the global and not just local environment – and, from a pragmatic perspective, to develop skills that would enable them to be players in the globalised world of the 21st century. Pragmatically too, the development of programmes that had international recognition and were offered in many different schools around the world enabled those with transient, globally-mobile employment to move as a family without having to worry about disruption to their children's education through frequent moves between education systems. And not only has the development of the IB programmes been influential for those who adopt a globally-mobile lifestyle. The increasing awareness within national education systems of the need to prepare young citizens for a future where the lives of those who remain within national boundaries will be influenced by factors from beyond these boundaries has come about to some extent because of ideas raised through the IB, as demand within national schools has increased not only for more internationalised education systems but also for the IB programmes themselves.

For those with an interest in the IB and the concept of an international curriculum this compendium will undoubtedly be of value. It will be of no less value to those with an interest in organisational development and change, as a case study of how the good idea of a small group of volunteers can be translated into a worldwide organisation, all the while responding to the challenges presented in operating in a multilingual and multicultural context surrounded by the shifting sands of political, economic and technological developments. It would be easy to forget, given the place the IB holds today, that the road to its current achievements has at times been rocky and that on at least one occasion it seemed likely that the 'good idea' would not make it through to assured long term implementation. This compendium reminds us that the path to organisational success is rarely smooth, and that the success that is taken for granted some 40 years on may well have been hard won in earlier days.

To write any form of historical account is a challenging task. It is difficult to imagine any context in which all would share exactly the same view of events, as we each bring to any situation our own perspective influenced by previous experiences and current context. Ian Hill is better placed than most to engage in such a task. Prior to joining the IB as Regional Director for Africa, Europe and the Middle East in 1993, Ian had gained experience from his work in an education ministry in Australia and then as head of an IB bilingual school in France. He had thus seen the IB's value in the school context. His role as Regional Director brought him into contact with many different schools, students, parents and ministries, with his subsequent role as Deputy Director General (from 2000 to the present) providing insights into not only the internal workings of the IB organisation and the major changes it has undergone (not least the introduction of the MYP in 1994 and the PYP in 1997), but also the external influences and pressures on the developing organisation. The focus of his own PhD thesis – policy formulation in the IB, completed in 1994 – undoubtedly also provided a sound basis of knowledge and analysis for the task at hand. Indeed, the pains to which he has clearly gone in tracking down archive material from many different sources – no mean feat when the early days of any new venture are rarely systematically documented – and in arranging interviews with key players in the various stages of IB development, have borne fruit as we not only read the story of the IB but also see reference to the many sources upon which he has drawn for supporting evidence. Telling the story itself is, of course, no easy task in terms of decisions that need to be taken about what to include and what to leave out, and how to divide the story into manageable sections that stand alone in a meaningful way while at the same time linking together with a degree of coherence. In basing his account on a combination of the chronological and the thematic, Ian Hill has achieved a good balance in doing just that, while his own wide experience and personal perspective illustrated through comments and anecdotes serves to bring an additional human dimension to the unfolding story.

As the fourth compendium of articles written originally for the *International Schools Journal*, this collection differs from the earlier three (whose themes were ESL, Culture and the Classroom) in bringing together 14 themed articles written by the same author. In doing so, with its theme of the IB's early days and subsequent growth, the compendium complements earlier accounts of the IB's development, but also goes beyond them. Bringing together these articles in one place has undoubtedly made them more easily accessible to those with an interest in the IB. In reading this account, however, it is important to bear in mind that each chapter represents an article written originally somewhere between 2001 and 2008. The comments and observations must thus be read as comments and observations from that time, without the benefit of the hindsight that comes to those of us reading them some years later. Expressions such as 'today' and 'currently' need to be interpreted against that backdrop. In just three places have updates been added at the time of editing. Where names are included of those holding the offices of Director General, President of the IB North America Board and Chair of the International Heads Representative Committee, footnotes have added updated details to avoid any appearance of factual inaccuracy.

For those with an academic interest in researching international education (who can at times be frustrated by the dearth of relevant sources available in this field) this compendium provides a mine of otherwise inaccessible facts, figures and explanations of how the IB – and international education more broadly – came to be where it is today. For those with a professional, rather than academic, interest it will equally provide a source of insight into the development of an organisation and the reasons why things are as they are (the origins of the schools' annual subscription described in Part X being an interesting case in point). Some aspects of the history may be unexpected. While it is no surprise, for instance, that the International School of Geneva, Atlantic College and the United Nations International School (UNIS) New York were centrally involved in the development of the IB diploma from the outset, how many of us were aware that North Manchester High School for Girls participated in the 1968 trial examinations? It is well known that the original establishment of the Diploma was followed by the IB's adoption of the International Schools Association Curriculum (ISAC) to form the Middle Years Programme in 1994, and the International Schools Curriculum Project (ISCP) in 1997 to form the Primary Years Programme. We may be surprised, then, to read that the earliest ideas for an international Leaving Certificate (the precursor of the Diploma) emanating from the International School of Geneva and the International Schools Association were complemented by a proposal for an international primary school curriculum, described in a document published in 1966 (and apparently unknown to the later instigators of the ISCP).

Reading this account will not only unearth such nuggets, but will also likely engender in readers an admiration for the early pioneers who had the 'good idea', who with courage and determination put energy, enthusiasm and time into persuading others of the 'good idea', and who managed to secure funding to enable that 'good idea' to be put into practice. We must also acknowledge the contribution made by the students who formed the early pilot groups of the IB Diploma Programme, the universities who were prepared to accept the early qualification, and those who put such efforts into persuading universities worldwide of its benefits. Acknowledgement, too, must be given to the ministries of education who gave the IB their support and, since those pioneering days, the many IB employees, examiners, teachers and other educators who have, at different stages and for varying lengths of time, contributed their skills to sustaining and developing the growing organisation. And last but by no means least, readers of this compendium owe a debt of gratitude to Ian Hill – not only for the central contribution he has made to the development of the IB over many years, but also for putting together these fascinating insights and sharing more widely the story of the IB. There are no doubt further challenges ahead for this organisation with its ambitious remit, as it grapples with expansion, with issues of access and cost, and with the very notion of what it means to be an international curriculum in the globalised world of the 21st century. In facing these challenges, those involved in developing and supporting the IB will surely be better equipped than they might otherwise have been if they engage with the insights this compendium provides of how the organisation came to be the influential player it is on today's global stage.

Mary Hayden

Part I – Early stirrings: the beginnings of the international education movement

Abstract

This chapter discusses the first proposals for international programmes and qualifications that preceded the creation of the International Baccalaureate (IB) Diploma Programme during the 1960s. A number of possible motivating factors are identified in an attempt to explain why this interest came about.

A *maturité internationale* – 1925

The Great War of 1914-1918 demonstrated in a terrible manner the way in which nations were distrustful and intolerant of each other. In the uneasy peace of the 1920s and 1930s, national leaders began the first tentative steps towards global cooperation, which were to result in the foundation of the United Nations. In 1920-21 the League of Nations and the International Labour Office established their headquarters in Geneva with staff drawn from many countries. There was a need for a school that would cater for students with a diversity of languages and cultures, a school that could prepare them for university education in their home countries. So it was that, in 1924, the International School of Geneva was founded by a group of parents predominantly from the League of Nations and the International Labour Office in conjunction with Adolphe Ferrière, a sociologist and educationist, and Elisabeth Rotten, a German scholar, both of the Rousseau Institute (1912) in Geneva. The parents, motivated by a belief in the objectives of the organisations they served, wanted a school that would give the child a complete and rounded view of the world, which was the workshop of his parents; not only the view, but the knowledge and understanding; not only knowledge, but the love and the desire for peace, the feeling of the brotherhood of man (Maurette 1948, p3).

Ferrière housed the first class in his family's chalet and was technical adviser to the school from 1924 to 1926, during which time the Rousseau Institute launched the International Bureau of Education with Piaget as its first director and Ferrière as assistant director (Avanzini *et al* 1979, p44). Ferrière was a prolific writer on sociology and education and had championed the New School movement, which he interpreted as promoting spontaneous, activity-based teaching with manual work – responding to the students' needs and personal experiences rather than closely following textbooks – and providing moral education through student self-government of schools. He found few enthusiasts for his ideas; the teachers and parents of the new international school in Geneva were not interested either (Hameline 1985-86, p382).

The school's objectives were to meet the specific educational demands of 'an international community such as exists in Geneva ... to imbue the new school community in which the students were to live and grow with an earnest belief in "internationalism"' (*International School of Geneva Student-Parent Handbook* 1924). There was also an important practical aspect to the initiative: the programmes of the school should enable students to continue their studies in the schools and universities of other countries (Oats 1952, p2). The International School of Geneva is regarded as the first of the international schools; that is, a school offering curricula for a culturally varied student population. A Swiss, Paul Meyhoffer, was the first director of the school.

In 1925 Ferrière signed a letter with accompanying questionnaire sent to 17 European leaders in educational reform, seeking their comments on a proposed *maturité internationale*. (In Switzerland the secondary leaving certificate is still called the *maturité* and the *baccalauréat* exists in France). He signed it as the director of the International Office of New Schools (which he had established in 1899) and on behalf of the board of the International School of Geneva where the concept had been discussed (Ferrière 1925). This was the first known suggestion of an international school-leaving examination. The idea of a *maturité internationale* had arisen through parental concern over university acceptance of their children in other countries after completing studies at the International School of Geneva.

The proposal was for a minimum obligatory programme of seven disciplines – history, native language, geography, biology, physics, maths and a 'manual occupation' (which included the arts). At least two of the seven subjects were to be studied in more depth. Which ancient and modern languages should be taught was asked in a separate part of the questionnaire. Ferrière's New School philosophy is noticeable in the fifth question, which asks whether advice should not first be sought on teaching methodology and content using the expertise of the Rousseau Institute; this would enable an enquiry into the dominant interests of adolescents, into memory, will, emotions and temperaments, which would require different approaches.

There is no record of the responses. The call was perhaps too early as international schools had only just begun (Peterson 1987, p15). Nevertheless world geography and world history courses for primary and early high school were developed at the school during the 1930s by Monsieur Dupuy, a retired professor and pioneer of geography teaching from the Sorbonne, and his daughter,

Madame Maurette, Headmistress from 1929 to 1949 (Oats 1952, pp26-28).

The rise of international schools

Across the world in Japan a group of parents met in September 1924 to discuss the creation of a new school for the expatriate children within the Yokohama community. A Swiss, Dr Wild, was the first director and thereby the first chair of the board of trustees. Classes began in a rented room at the local YMCA in October, only a few weeks after the commencement of classes at the International School of Geneva. Both schools started with a handful of students and moved premises as enrolments grew. By 1929 parents at the Yokohama International School were criticising the curriculum for not responding to the needs of the diverse nationalities in the school, and for lacking structure and direction. The board then considered three systems: an English method of the Parents National Education Union (PNEU), American methods, and the 'continental European method used at the International School of Geneva'. In December 1929, the Swiss director, Dr Peter (who had replaced Dr Wild), asked the board to consider the creation of 'a truly international curriculum (for primary grades), consciously or unconsciously longed for by the progressive education of all countries' (Stanworth 1998, p43). He spoke of the need to promote international understanding, of collaborating with other schools working towards international ideals, and of the school, over time, becoming a centre for international education. This was too progressive for the board. It continued with an eclectic curriculum that leant more towards the English approach and Dr Peter resigned. A broader teaching of history and geography was, however, encouraged from 1930; could they have heard of the work of Dupuy and Maurette in Geneva? In 1936 the director encouraged a spirit of service for others to enhance personal development (a precursor of community service in the IB programmes?). In 1955 the school re-opened after the Second World War and became affiliated with the International Bureau of Education, Geneva. It has offered the International Baccalaureate (IB) Diploma Programme since 1986, after having made its first enquiries to Alec Peterson in 1970.

The League of Nations gave way to the United Nations (UN) Organisation, whose charter was established in San Francisco in 1945 and whose headquarters was (and still is) in New York. Its principal goal was to maintain world peace and thus avoid the tragedy of any further world wars. Just as the League of Nations' personnel had given birth to the International School of Geneva, so did UN employees become instrumental parents in founding the United Nations International School (UNIS) in New York in 1947. Unlike the League of Nations, the UN gave substantial grants to the school during its first 25 years (Malinowski & Zorn 1973, p164).

A number of schools sprang up in different parts of the world under the diplomatic umbrella of one or more embassies. For example, the Djakarta International Primary School (Indonesia) was founded in 1951 with assistance from the American Embassy; Kabul International Primary School was founded in 1954 in Afghanistan under the aegis of the French Embassy; and the International School of Ghana in Accra was founded in 1955 under the patronage of 'seven ambassadorial officers with the active sponsorship of the Ghana Ministry of Education' (Knight & Leach 1964, p449-450).

The end of the Second World War saw the decline of the British Empire and the emergence of the USA as a world power. Many former colonies became individual states and the nations of Europe began to unite for common economic and political ends. With the approaching end of colonisation in the late 1950s, there were many displaced nationals on various missions, technical aid or business in countries throughout the world.

Rapid air travel, telecommunications, the electronic computer and the rise of information technology all contributed to the development of a world that was increasingly interdependent and international. Many industrial companies, which formerly had a predominately national role, took on multinational dimensions in this new political and technological climate.

UNESCO was formed in 1945, after the end of the Second World War, with its headquarters in Paris, to promote international, intellectual cooperation in the fields of education, science and culture. Another UN specialised agency, the World Health Organisation (WHO), was created at the same time in Geneva and others followed in the years to come. These represent important political, social and ideological factors that added to the international displacement of national public servants.

After the Second World War, international education exchanges between the USA, Europe and the Middle East occurred. The USA government launched itself into 'bilateral internationalism' by supporting student exchanges, particularly at university level. Many foreign students studied at universities and colleges in the USA and the 1946 Fulbright Act allowed many Americans to study overseas (Leach 1969a, p132). In 1950 UNESCO sponsored teacher exchanges across the world in conjunction with the Conference of Internationally-Minded Schools (CIS), which is discussed later. These factors contributed to the growth of international schools to serve the rapidly expanding population of students residing in countries other than that of their first nationality.

At the same time, in the Europe of post-Second World War, international schools were appearing in part to serve foreign personnel in cities such as

Copenhagen, Frankfurt and Paris (Fox 1985, p54). During the late 1950s and 1960s developing countries received a substantial influx of foreign aid, investment and expatriate families – who needed an education that would enable their children to easily reintegrate into their national education systems or to systems in other countries; this economic factor also contributed to the growth of international schools in a number of places around the globe.

The constant mobility and cultural displacement of students was not assisted by variations of curricula and the divergence of university entrance requirements. The nationally diverse populations of international schools, while providing a rich, cultural experience, also led to a number of problems.

A UNESCO international diploma – 1946 and 1948

The Collège Cévénol, a boarding school in a fairly remote area of central France, was founded as an international school in 1938 by two protestant ministers, Messieurs Trocmé and Theis. They had hidden many Jews during the Second World War in and around their school at Chambon-sur-Lignon, and had accepted students displaced from other countries, by the ravages of war, into their school. A sense of idealism for world peace was behind their actions and at the base of the school's philosophy. They supported student exchanges as a means of facilitating intercultural understanding.

A second call for a common pre-university qualification across the world to facilitate the student exchanges came from Theis (the Headmaster) and Trocmé. They sought political acceptance for the idea from higher places in post-war France and the Minister for Education gave his support. The November 1946 *Handbook* of the school contains the following statement by the then Minister for Education, André Philip:

> *On sent de plus en plus la nécessité d'orienter l'enseignement secondaire dans le sens des écoles internationales. Celles-ci devraient pouvoir délivrer un diplôme à caractère international, sanctionné par l'UNESCO, comportant une équivalence avec les diplômes correspondants de chaque nation.*

> [The necessity for secondary teaching to align itself with international schools is felt more and more. These schools should be able to deliver an international diploma authorised by UNESCO and having equivalent status with the corresponding diplomas of each nation.] (Collège Cévénol *Handbook*, November 1946).

This idea was to be reiterated by Theis and Trocmé three years later at a landmark meeting at UNESCO in Paris.

In 1948 Mr Kees Boeke, director of the Werkplaats International Children's Community in Bilthoven (Holland), persuaded the education division of UNESCO of the importance of support for international schools (Oats 1950, p1). Boeke wrote to the assistant director-general of education, UNESCO, proposing a world institution with branches in various countries so that children of all nationalities could be educated for world citizenship through international student exchanges, which would eventually require an international diploma.

It will be necessary for reaching success that an international diploma be awarded as a result of the coordinated studies completed in different branches of the world institution and that this diploma is recognised for entrance in the universities of various countries (Boeke 1948).

Conference of Principals of International Schools – 1949

UNESCO was interested at the time in the mutual appreciation of various cultures and was concerned that progress be made in this direction. As a result UNESCO convened a 'Conference of Principals of International Schools' on 31st March/1st April 1949 at its headquarters in Paris; this was attended by the Heads of 15 schools wishing to develop an international outlook.

The list of invitations to the first meeting was compiled by Kees Boeke who had had previous contact with a number of internationally-minded educators. Dr Kurt Hahn of Gordonstoun School, Scotland (who later founded the United World College movement where the IB is taught almost exclusively); Madame Hatinguais of the Centre International d'Etudes Pédagogiques at Sèvres (an important French influence in the development of the IB); Monsieur Roquette of the International School of Geneva (where the first IB curricula were conceived); and the Prince of Hannover from Salem School, Germany (previously directed by Kurt Hahn), were four of the most distinguished educators at the meeting. Other schools in Holland (Quakerschool, Eerde-Ommen), England (Dartington Hall and Badminton School), Switzerland (Pestalozzi Children's Village), Scotland, Germany (Odenwaldschule), France (Collège Cévénol), Sweden (Viggbyholmsskolan) and the USA were represented. Dr F Hackett from Riverdale Country School (USA) was the only non-European present. (Three of these schools later adopted the IB diploma course: the International School of Geneva, Salem School and the Collège Cévénol.) In addition there were four observers, including Mr C H Dobinson, Reader in Education at Oxford, whose department of education was later to play an important administrative and pedagogical role in the development of the IB (through Bill Halls and Alec Peterson). UNESCO provided the venue, full secretarial assistance and translators. As Dr Cheng Chi-Pao, acting head of the education department of UNESCO observed in his opening address, this was the *first* such meeting concerning international education ever to be held. It established contacts that were later to be important for the development of the IB Diploma Programme.

Two major items were discussed at this first meeting: Boeke's idea of an international educational institution offering an international diploma with branches all over the world to facilitate student exchanges (and thus promote international understanding), and the desperate need to train teachers in international schools, which was raised by Monsieur Roquette. A subcommittee of the inaugural meeting, chaired by Roquette, organised the first ever Course for Teachers Interested in International Education in 1950 at the International School of Geneva.

Boeke discussed the need for an international diploma for which government recognition was to be obtained in different countries, thus enabling students to study in universities all over the world. At the first CIS meeting Monsieur Theis of the Collège Cévénol spoke of the serious obstacle to student exchanges caused by the rigidity of prescribed national curricula and university entrance requirements:

> Monsieur Theis hoped very much indeed that an international diploma could be instituted which would in time be accepted for entrance to all or most of the universities of the world (Conference of Principals of International Schools, Minutes 1949, p9).

The meeting agreed in principle but felt that the task was too demanding for their group and that an organisation such as UNESCO might be able to take it up. (A preliminary statement was available from a study of university entrance requirements already undertaken by the International Association of Professors and Lecturers with financial assistance from UNESCO.)

Nevertheless the genuine interest of the meeting in Theis' and Boeke's idea is reflected in a compromise resolution from Roquette whereby all schools present 'should experiment in 1950 with the award of an international diploma at the end of secondary school in addition to the regular diploma' (Conference of Principals of International Schools, Minutes 1949, p10). Each school was to be free to make its own regulations for this diploma, but two aspects were essential: 'satisfactory' knowledge of a language other than the student's own and the preparation of a mini-thesis on a subject of world significance. Were these the dawnings of the foreign language and extended essay requirements of the IB diploma? The minutes of subsequent meetings contain no follow-up to this resolution.

The Conference of Internationally-Minded Schools (CIS)

This was followed by a second meeting in 1951 where the CIS was then founded and UNESCO later agreed to continue to convene an annual meeting. The geographical distribution of schools at this meeting was greater than for the 1949 meeting. Twenty participants representing schools in the following countries were present: France, Germany, Holland, Hong Kong, India, Jordan, Scotland, Switzerland, USA. Considering that travel and communication across the globe was of the pre-jet and pre-fax era, it was a noteworthy achievement to bring together people from schools outside Europe – America, Asia and the Middle East.

Membership was open to schools that 'consciously aim at furthering world peace and international understanding through education' (Report of the Second Conference of Principals of International Schools and Schools Specially Interested in Developing International Understanding 1951). The association was legally constituted in the country of its secretariat to collect funds for its purposes. Mr Frank Button of Badminton School, England, was the first secretary. A membership fee of not less than £1 for individuals and £5 for schools was struck. In addition to providing a venue and secretarial assistance, UNESCO funded a number of projects for the CIS during its lifetime. It brought together Heads mainly from national schools in Europe, with an increasing interest from American schools. The aims of the association were:

1. To provide training for teachers in international schools.

2. To foster student exchanges via a network of internationally-minded schools across the world

3. To work towards recognition of the equivalence of university entrance diplomas in all countries and the development of international diplomas for university acceptance everywhere.

(Report of the Second Conference of Principals of International Schools and Schools Specially Interested in Developing International Understanding 1951).

The CIS met annually in April at UNESCO, organised workshops for teachers in different places and provided three publications:

- *CIS Bulletin* – three times a year in English and French;

- *International School Magazine* – three times per year, produced by students and a teacher at the International School of Geneva for some years; and

• reports of teacher workshops.

It was the third organisation (after the International School of Geneva and the Collège Cévénol) to sow the seeds for an international qualification. The CIS continued to meet annually at UNESCO House in Paris and concentrated on providing international student exchanges and training for teachers in international schools, until its amalgamation with the International Schools Association occurred in 1969 (ISA 1968).

Leadership of CIS was vested in the usual office-bearers of an association: president, vice-president, secretary, treasurer and executive committee members. Roquette (Headmaster of the International School of Geneva) was the first president. His emphasis was on training teachers for international schools. Two members of the executive committee – Boeke (Holland) and Theis (France) – were the people who, according to the minutes (and Boeke's letter to UNESCO), wished to promote student exchange, coordination of curricula across the globe and a common pre-university diploma.

As an organisation, CIS played no further role in proposing or working towards an international university qualification; the third aim, then, lapsed. However, two CIS members – Desmond Cole-Baker of the International School of Geneva and Madame Hatinguais of the French Ministry of Education – were to become important actors in the development of the IB diploma. The inaugural meeting of school Heads in 1949 led to a conference for teachers in the following year to discuss matters surrounding the three aims of the CIS. The debate on international education had formally begun.

Part II – The beginnings of the international education movement

Abstract

This chapter assumes a knowledge of Part I, which covered the period 1924-1951. It continues to identify early proposals for international programmes and qualifications from 1950 until 1962 when the development of the International Baccalaureate Diploma began. The following landmarks are discussed: a course for teachers interested in international education, the founding of the International Schools Association (ISA), the United Nations International School (UNIS), the European Baccalaureate, and the conference of teachers of social studies in international schools. A number of possible motivating factors are identified in an attempt to explain why these events took place and to underline their importance in the evolution of the concept of international education.

The educational programmes of international schools

As international schools started to grow in many parts of the world, the most pressing problem was that of preparing senior students for university, either in their home country or elsewhere, and of facilitating international exchange or transfer of students at various stages of schooling. An international academic passport was required. Confronted with a diverse cultural mix of students, what should the academic programme be?

Some international schools prepared all students for the one national examination and relied upon 'equivalence' agreements (which were not always easy to negotiate) to secure university placements in other countries. For example, the UWC of the Atlantic in Wales offered only A levels when it was founded in 1962, yet its students came from all over the world (Peterson 1968, p274). Others prepared a number of national examinations within the one school such as the International School of the Hague (later to become the American School of the Hague), founded in 1953, where three national streams operated leading to the pre-university examinations of France, Germany and the USA (Knight & Leach 1964, p452). UNIS, New York, offered American Advanced Placement (AP) and A levels from England (Malinowski & Zorn 1973, p128). From the outset the International School of Geneva prepared students for the national university entrance examinations of England (A levels), France (*baccalauréat*), Germany (*arbitur*), Switzerland (*maturité*), and later (in the 1940s) the American College Board AP examinations (Mowat 1968, p280). At the International School of Geneva after the Second World War there were small numbers of students undertaking courses in classes grouped according to nationality. A similar situation existed or would soon exist in other international schools such as UNIS. This led to economic difficulties and cultural isolation – perhaps the same difficulties as those that had prompted Ferrière's call for an international university entrance examination in 1925.

Teachers were also concerned about the inappropriateness of national curricula for providing a truly global dimension and international experience in the academic programme. The informal relationships between culturally diverse individuals in an international school setting should be enhanced by formal recognition in the academic programme of subjects, methodological approaches and international comparisons that would enable individuals to see their own cultural identity in relation to the rest of the world. Such a programme would go a long way towards teaching tolerance of other ways of thinking and being, and would contribute to world peace through mutual understanding amongst nations, a theme that was prevalent after the First and Second World Wars. Pedagogical problems could arise where, for example, mathematical procedures and thought processes or the perception of historical events vary between nations. This could lead to difficult conflicts within the individual who transfers from one system to another, particularly if national programmes do not allow for culturally different approaches.

Referring to the multicultural and transitory nature of international school students, one writer described international schools as 'veritable towers of Babel filled with adolescent nomads' for whom an international programme and worldwide university access were indispensable (Hanson 1971, p10).

'Course for teachers interested in international education' – 1950
This four week summer course at the International School of Geneva was organised on behalf of (what was to become after 1951) the Conference of Internationally Minded Schools (CIS). It had been suggested by Fred Roquette at the 1949 meeting in Paris (Conference of Principals of International Schools: Minutes 1949). He was assisted by W (Bill) Oats, the Australian Quaker who had returned to the school in 1949 from his position as Headmaster of the Friends School, Hobart, Tasmania, now an IB diploma school (Oats 1950 & 1952). The conference was financed by a grant of US$1000 from UNESCO and participants paid their own travel and board.

The 50 participants comprised teachers and some Headmasters from international schools in Australia, Belgium, Ceylon, Denmark, England, France, Germany, Greece, Holland, Hong Kong, India, Ireland, Italy, Luxembourg, Norway, Pakistan, Switzerland and the USA. Kees Boeke from the Children's

Community in Bilthoven was there. The discussion group *animateurs* were: Roquette, Oats, Boeke, Louis Johannot (director of the Institut 'Le Rosey', Switzerland), Miss Mary Wilson (warden of Women's Hall of Residence, University College of North Staffs, Keele, England) and Miss Louise Wood (one of the directors of the International Quaker Centre, Paris). This gathering of teachers occurred because of a common desire to discuss how schooling could be made more international both in content and teaching methodology; the motivating forces were educational, cultural (there was much discussion about exposing students to other ways of life) and ideological ('internationalising' schooling would contribute to world peace).

By the end of the course, agreement on a definition of international education was reached:

> It should give the child an understanding of his past as a common heritage to which all men irrespective of nation, race, or creed have contributed and which all men should share; it should give him an understanding of his present world as a world in which peoples are interdependent and in which cooperation is a necessity.
>
> In such an education emphasis should be laid in a basic attitude of respect for all human beings as persons, understanding of those things which unite us and an appreciation of the positive values of those things which may seem to divide us, with the objective of thinking free from fear or prejudice (Final Report of the Course for Teachers Interested in International Education 1950: Section I).

This is probably the first known definition of international education; it is the first devised by a group of educators from different countries meeting together. (Comenius, in the 17th century, is regarded as a pre-cursor of international education with his proposed international organisation of research and education, and in the 18th century Voltaire's Micromégas travelled from planet to planet to develop his mind and his heart.)

In response to Kees Boeke's proposal of a worldwide network of schools with common curricula to facilitate an international exchange of students, the Final Report expresses reservations about a chain of international boarding schools based chiefly on the lack of a real family life in living away from home. Such students would also become disoriented without a country or a religion. Of most importance for this study is the comment concerning an international exam:

> We do not think that it is possible or even desirable to unify school programs and final secondary school exams on an international basis. They depend to a large extent on the needs of each country (Report of

26

the Course for Teachers Interested in International Education, Final Report 1950: Section II).

A fear of losing national identity and not accommodating local educational imperatives through conforming to common programmes seems to be at the root of this statement. The size of the task may also have been a deterrent. Desmond Cole-Baker remarked that 'an internationally acceptable university entrance examination was raised by the CIS but the task was considered too enormous' (Cole-Baker 1990, p38). Participants in this course did, however, want an international curriculum perspective, particularly in history. It was not until the Conference of Social Studies Teachers met in 1962 that the idea of common curricula and examinations was again considered as a way towards university access and the provision of an international curriculum perspective.

The Final Report went on to address the following issues: international training of teachers, international interchange between schools and teachers, relations with education authorities, collaboration of parents and colleagues in international education, the teaching of foreign languages and literature, national characteristics to be presented in international education, and religious instruction in international education. Many resolutions on these matters were taken up by the CIS.

The negative response to an international diploma was noted by the CIS (Conference of Principals of International Schools and Schools Specially Interested in Developing International Understanding: Report of the Second Meeting 1951), and the idea was dropped by that association altogether but was revived almost ten years later by a sister organisation – the International Schools Association (ISA). Similar courses continued in the form of CIS professional development programmes for teachers in various disciplines almost annually thereafter in conjunction with UNESCO. This kept alive the discussion on international education launched by the first meeting of school Heads in 1949.

International Schools Association (ISA) – 1951
The CIS brought together 'schools of countries affected by the Second World War. These were mainly national schools of the private category but did include the International School of Geneva' (Cole-Baker 1990, p37). The ISA, on the other hand, was created in 1951 by parents who were international civil servants in Geneva, New York and Paris, all of whom were initially members of school governing boards. These people saw a need to link schools serving the children of international public servants, that is schools with a diversity of expatriate nationalities amongst the student population, whereas CIS membership consisted almost exclusively of internationally-*minded* Heads of national

schools. Moreover the parents, acting out of ideology for world peace and cooperation (stemming from the UN organisations where they were employed) and family welfare concerns for their own children, wanted an association in which parents could take a lead. Headmasters of international schools did attend ISA meetings, but UN civil servants were the initial driving force and continued as active executive officers for the first 25 years.

The chairman and instigator of the inaugural meeting of the 20th of November 1951 at UNESCO House, Paris, was Bertram Pickard, also chairman of the governing board of the International School of Geneva. Members of this board were UN officials who hoped to develop close relations with and support from UNESCO (Leach 1969a, p16). Pickard already knew of the existence of CIS as Roquette (who attended the inaugural ISA meeting) had attended the first meeting of what was to become the CIS in 1949. The organisation was initially called the International Schools Liaison Committee and became the International Schools Association (ISA) from the third meeting. The inaugural gathering consisted of representatives from four schools associated with the UN plus some advisers as follows:

School Representatives

International School of Geneva	B Pickard, board chair
	F Roquette, director
UN Nursery School (Geneva)	Mrs M Crump, director
UNIS (New York)	L Steinig, board chair
	Miss J Henderson,
	board vice-chair
UN Nursery School (Paris)	Mrs G Grauss, director
	Mrs K Delavernay,
	board chair

Advisers

R Cook, UN Geneva, member of the International School of Geneva board

H Abraham, Department of Education, UNESCO

R Lenz, legal advisor

Mrs A Myrdal

(International Schools Liaison Committee Minutes, 20 November 1951)

When the second meeting took place in 1952 the three chief executive offices were filled by UN employees who were also parents:

Chairman: R Cook, UN Geneva, board member of the International

School of Geneva
Secretary: Dr W Wall, chairman of education committee, UNESCO Staff Association
Treasurer: F Wilson, World Health Organisation (Geneva), board member UN Nursery School, Geneva
(International Schools Liaison Committee Minutes, 6 December 1952)

For practical reasons the ISA met thereafter at the International School of Geneva when UN officials from New York and Paris gathered there for other meetings. ISA had consultative status with UNESCO and its secretariat was established in Geneva. Participating schools paid an annual subscription.

After the inaugural meeting, and until December 1952, Fred Roquette (director of the International School of Geneva) was ISA chairman. This short chairmanship was followed by that of Russell Cook, a member of the governing board of the International School of Geneva and a UN public servant at the World Health Organisation. He was the longest-serving chairman of ISA – for 18 years from December 1952 to August 1970. Russell Cook was to be an influential individual and the ISA an indispensable organisation in the development of the IB Diploma Programme.

In 1955 ISA formed the International Schools Foundation based in New York with the purpose of 'raising money for international schools' (ISA 1968a). This became International Schools Services, a private, non-profit organisation currently housed in Princeton, New Jersey, to serve American international schools overseas.

The ISA was established to fulfill four purposes:

• to develop close cooperation between existing international schools by means of regular or occasional consultations on educational or administrative questions;

• to stimulate, facilitate or carry out research work on educational or administrative questions;

• to promote the establishment of new international schools; and

• to publicise aims and principles of international schools.
(ISA 1957)

The provision of an internationally recognised common curriculum and examination later arose from the first two purposes.

The organisation was registered with articles of association under Swiss law. Its constitution proscribed any single national dominance in the governance of its member schools. An *ISA Bulletin* was published four to five times a year.

While Headmasters participated more as time went on, executive control for some years was largely in the hands of parents (with good intentions) who wielded considerable power due to their triple leverage:

1. their elected executive status in ISA;

2. their standing as elected members or executive officers of school governing boards (to whom the Headmasters were responsible); and

3. their rank as highly-placed employees in UN organisations or embassies, which gave them considerable political clout on an international level.

Since school boards hire and fire Headmasters, the ISA was not, therefore, a gathering of colleagues of equal status. Moreover, the influential status of these parents could hinder or advance the cause of 'internationalism'. For instance, Cole-Baker's initiative to assess the needs of international schools by appointing an ISA consultant was not well received by Russell Cook and other executive officers according to the consultant (Leach 1991). The same opinion is expressed by Cole-Baker:

> The ISA was remarkable in that it was established by non-academics and no teacher sat on its Executive Committee. ...I needed an umbrella for this project [assessing the needs of international schools] so I decided to try and open up the ISA. This was traumatic as we had to remove a number of well-intentioned gentlemen and get headmasters playing an active part in the organisation (Cole-Baker 1989).

The leverage of the parents was finally, however, a positive aid to the establishment of the IB Diploma Programme.

The United Nations International School (UNIS), New York – 1947
From the day it opened in 1947 the parents and staff of UNIS emphasized an international dimension in curriculum planning. The first objective for the new primary curriculum stated:

> To try to give the child a sound education which, while preserving his native tongue, history and cultural background, will, at the same time, in the work and play of the school free him of those prejudices and pieces of misinformation which separate peoples; so that wherever he may be in the future, he remains a good citizen of his own country, more important, a good citizen of the world (Malinowski & Zorn 1973, p24).

In practice there were inevitable tensions in arriving at a balance between the

30

idealistic and utilitarian aims of the curriculum; parents needed to be reassured that the creation of UNIS's own international curriculum would not make it difficult for students to fit into national systems in other countries. This was more acutely felt as the school grew into the senior secondary years where university entry required recognised national qualifications; would a UNIS leaving qualification be accepted? It took some years, but the balance was achieved. UNIS commenced with English and French language streams and with no written curriculum; teachers were given general aims and objectives and had to develop their approach and content from those. (Unlike the International School of Geneva in French-speaking Switzerland, UNIS was unable to sustain the French stream in an English-speaking country.)

During the first few years, an education committee of the governing board gave emphasis to the development of the social studies programme. It considered material produced by UNESCO on the teaching of geography (Ficheux *et al* 1949) and history (Hill 1953) for international understanding together with the work of Madame Maurette (Maurette 1948) from the International School of Geneva who had participated in the drafting of UNIS's 'Preliminary Programme' statements in 1947. The committee also consulted the educational programme of the State of New York. The resulting 1954 social studies curriculum was high on international understanding but not easy to put into practice, through lack of textbooks without a national bias and lack of teachers trained in the delivery of international curricula.

In 1955 the Ford Foundation agreed to provide, through its Fund for the Advancement of Education, US$85,000 for the development of international curricula by UNIS. This was to assist with the expenses of planning for the future of the school and for a study of the application that might be made in the USA of the experience of UNIS. It was a primary school at the time, and had developed an international primary curriculum. It commenced its first junior high school year in 1955, not reaching grade 12 until 1961-1962. The grant was timely to allow UNIS to develop a secondary international programme. The Ford Foundation continued to play a significant part in funding international education projects, including that of the IB Diploma Programme.

The executive committee minutes of 1949 contain the first mention of the creation of a UNIS leaving diploma, which would be recognised internationally for university entrance; this was quite independent from the call for an international leaving diploma (for use by many schools), which the Heads of internationally-minded schools made in Paris in the same year. The senior school curriculum was to include the best features of the leading education systems of the world 'ascertained through the careful study of entrance requirements for universities of the highest standards' (Malinowski & Zorn

31

1973, p120). In 1952 the chair of the education committee stated the need for UNIS to build an outstanding reputation so that its final diploma would be accepted by all universities. In 1958 the governing board reaffirmed its intention to establish a UNIS international diploma that would include at least a second language, world history, world geography, and the international character of maths and science where students were required to work with different national measures.

In 1962 Mr Aleck Forbes, the new director of UNIS, proposed 'pre-university department' courses of two to three years culminating in either GCE A levels or the American Advanced Placement (AP) exams. The idea of a UNIS diploma for international recognition had not been abandoned but the immediate needs of the students had to be met. Forbes and his staff then became interested in the ideas stemming from the International School of Geneva after the 1962 conference of teachers of social studies (see below). From that time UNIS worked collaboratively with the Geneva school and others towards the development of the International Baccalaureate (IB) for the last two years of secondary education. UNIS introduced the trial IB in September 1967, and before the end of the 1969-70 school year was one of five schools that decided to adopt it and phase out nearly all teaching of national curricula (Malinowski & Zorn 1973, p166).

The influence of the European Baccalaureate – 1959
In 1956 the ISA discussed the need for establishing equivalence amongst the various university entrance examinations. One idea was to seek acceptance from as many countries as possible for pupils holding a certificate covering equivalent school work (ISA 1956). The European Community had devised its own solution, which helped revive interest in an international pre-university examination. A lawyer with no initial connection to ISA, Dr Albert Van Houtte, co-founded the European Schools in 1957. He was invited to address an ISA meeting in 1959 about the European Baccalaureate Examination, which was offered for the first time in the same year (*Ecole Européenne: Informations Générales* 1991, p1). It is a common examination allowing transfer of students to universities of the participating countries.

Dr Van Houtte pressed the ISA to look seriously at an international university entrance examination for international schools that would extend beyond the European Baccalaureate (ISA 1959). Mayer incorrectly attributes Van Houtte's speech as the first attempt to push for an international university entrance examination when in fact it was Ferrière in 1925 (Ferrière 1925). He goes on to say that few international schools were preparing students for university at that time, so the topic was forgotten for a few years (Mayer 1968, p215). The advent of the European Baccalaureate strengthened the educational context in terms of the awareness of curricula and examinations that promoted international mobility.

Conference of teachers of social studies in international schools – 1962

In 1960 Mr Aleck Forbes, co-director of the International School of Geneva, at an ISA annual meeting, proposed that ISA should arrange a conference on the philosophy and international concepts of the social sciences up to the final secondary year. John Goormaghtigh, as treasurer of ISA, said that for 50 years the Carnegie Endowment (of which he was director for Europe) had been interested in the teaching of social sciences as a means to furthering international understanding, and he wholeheartedly agreed with the idea. Russell Cook suggested the International School of Geneva as the venue. Support was also forthcoming from representatives of a number of schools including the International School of Brussels, Stichting International School (the Hague), UNIS (New York), Ghana International School and the International School of Belgrade (ISA 1960). An *ad hoc* committee, chaired by a parent, was immediately formed to organise the event and a plan was submitted and approved by the ISA the next day.

Experts on cultural relations and social studies would be asked to speak to teachers from international schools. Requests for expert lecturers were sent to UNESCO, the director of the European College (Bruges), International Bureau of Education (Geneva), the Fulbright Organisation and the National Professional Teachers' Associations of Social Sciences in a number of countries in Europe, Africa, the Middle East and America. This conference was to have been held in 1961 but eventually took place in 1962 with the assistance of a small grant from UNESCO. Some school administrators attended but the majority of participants were teachers. The conference had the following published purposes:

- to discuss aims and objectives of teaching social sciences in international schools;

- to draw up syllabuses for teaching cross-cultural knowledge; and

- to rethink ideas and attitudes expressed in international schools in the light of international ideals and the multinational student.

All participants, including Forbes as the new director of UNIS (New York), provided reports on how social sciences were taught from grades 3 to 12 in their own international schools. The conference made the following recommendation:

The Conference asks ISA to issue a statement of educational aims acceptable to all member schools. It further requests that the development of a joint Social Studies final exam be explored by ISA as the first step toward the establishment of basic standards (First Conference of Teachers of Social Studies in International Schools: Report 1962, p5).

This outcome spurred the ISA Eleventh General Assembly (which took place at the same time) to recommend that the International School of Geneva take steps to:

- formulate an advanced level ISA examination in contemporary history (and political and economic affairs) to be jointly sponsored by English GCE, French Baccalaureate and American College Board officials; and

- develop common standards for grading and marking systems (ISA 1962).

These proposals were put into practice.

This gathering was a milestone in the maturation of the concept of international education and the catalyst for the development of the IB Diploma Programme.

Part III – The dawning of the IB diploma

Abstract

Part II covered the period 1950-1962. This chapter explores the intense activity in the early 1960s, centred on the International School of Geneva and the ISA, which marked the beginnings of the IB diploma. The independent curriculum development work for a programme of international education at Atlantic College is also discussed. Key figures – Blackburn, Cole-Baker, Goormaghtigh, Leach, Peterson – are identified, together with the events that led to their involvement.

Introduction

The ISA was the conduit for the recommendation from the 1962 'conference of teachers of social studies in international schools' that a social studies final exam be developed as a first step towards common standards. This led to the creation of the contemporary history course for international schools, and then other subjects, to form the IB diploma. The initial work was undertaken by teachers at the International School of Geneva, rightly considered the place where the IB diploma was spawned. Robert Leach's work as ISA consultant and curriculum developer is given special attention.

The reader will remember in Part II that UNIS in New York had been grappling with curricula for international education since its founding in 1947. Together with Atlantic College in Wales, which was established in 1962, these were among the first schools outside Geneva whose independent efforts in this area of education brought them into the exciting IB project. The chapter finishes with a tribute to John Goormaghtigh who, from the very beginning, gave so much of his voluntary time over such a long period to the IB.

Report of the ISA consultant Robert Leach – 1962

The focal point of the ISA's charter was to assist international schools throughout the world. At the ISA Tenth Assembly in July 1961, Desmond Cole-Baker, head of the English language section of the International School of Geneva, offered to release a senior staff member, Robert Leach (in charge of the history department) as consultant to ISA (International School of Geneva, Board Minutes 4 June 1962). The International School of Geneva provided US$7000 in advance to ISA for the consultant's expenses.

Leach acknowledges the foresight, commitment to international education and support given him by Cole-Baker: 'He is one of the few good administrators

I've seen. He knew how to delegate, how to get things done.' (Leach 1991b) His project was to visit international schools in Asia, Africa and Europe during the 1961-1962 school year and to gauge their interest in an international curriculum. More specifically he was to:

- assist with 'know how' accumulated at the International School of Geneva;
- gather questions to which ISA might provide solutions; and
- link the schools visited.

(ISA 1961)

At the same time Leach was able to promote the impending conference for teachers of social studies.

There is a clear reference in his report to the ideological mission of international schools, to unite people of different cultural backgrounds and to provide an education that would prepare students for world citizenship. The potentially restrictive nature of national curricula for international students, and the division into cultural groups to undertake national examinations within the one school, work against the pedagogical and ideological objectives of international schools. Of course international schools also had a utilitarian aim that was essential for their existence: to provide an education for the internationally mobile students where the national system of the host country was inappropriate, often because the teaching was in a language other than English – the predominant language of international schools. (United World Colleges are the exception; they are based on ideological motives only. They deliberately bring students of many nationalities together to promote world peace and international understanding with the IB diploma as the formal curriculum vehicle.)

The following extracts from Leach's report are pertinent since the term 'international baccalaureate' appears for the first time:

> Until an international baccalaureate is operative, the essential ideal of the international school falls down in practice (Leach 1962, p3).
> ... the development of an international baccalaureate has no value in itself as one more examination system. Its virtue lies in the good influence which it will bring in diminishing the divisive pull of national examination requirements (Leach 1962, p7).

Throughout Asia, Africa and Europe, Leach found international schools unanimous in believing that a leaving qualification with international acceptability was vital for their success (Leach 1991a), although this was only one of three needs that became apparent. The other two were that international schools required a great deal of assistance with curriculum development and with administrative restructuring. 'The isolation of many schools was terrible to see.' (Cole-Baker 1989)

Leach was an important actor in shaping the problems for which the IB was to be the eventual solution. As head of history and a well-travelled American Quaker, Leach had credibility. 'He saw the practical necessity for an IB; a national curriculum perspective, particularly in history, offended him intellectually. He was respected and liked by his students.' (Hanson 1992) Leach, after his ISA one year consultancy, wanted to return to the classroom and his post as head of history at the International School of Geneva, where he continued to regale students with his dynamic lessons until his retirement.

The International School of Geneva offered four national programmes as a response to the problem of university entrance. This had the following drawbacks:

- it created uneconomically viable class sizes;
- it clashed directly with the ethos of international schools by separating students into national groups;
- students still had difficulties being accepted by a number of universities when they held a national school qualification not of the country in which they wished to study; and
- in addition to the disparities between national systems of education (even *within* national systems), curricula and methods intended for a national community were often inappropriate to the socio-pedagogical needs of an international community.

(Renaud 1975, p112)

These same problems were applicable to other international schools as confirmed by Leach's report.

ISA makes a historic recommendation – 1962

There were two formal representations to the ISA during 1962 that set the agenda for the ISA decision to investigate the possibility of an international university-entrance diploma. The first was the ISA consultant's report. This had been sent to over 150 schools and individuals as a newsletter *before* the concurrent meetings of the ISA General Assembly and the Conference for Teachers of Social Studies in International Schools, which took place from the 26th August to the 1st September 1962 at the International School of Geneva (ISA 1962).

The second representation was the articulation of a need by the Conference for Teachers of Social Studies in International Schools for the development of an international examination for university entrance with a 'joint social studies final examination ... as the first step toward the establishment of basic standards' (First Conference of Teachers of Social Studies in International Schools: Report 1962, p5). This recommendation was reached during the first two days of the conference and was taken the next day to the ISA Eleventh Assembly, which was meeting at the same time. The ISA responded immediately by asking the International School of Geneva to prepare an international course in history as a first step towards common standards and a graduation certificate for use by its member schools. ISA turned to the school in Geneva because it provided an educational infrastructure with the expertise and willingness to undertake such a project. Moreover an important part of the ISA executive also sat on the board of the International School of Geneva.

During his term as ISA consultant, Leach had suggested an international examination in 1961 to Leo Fernig, a UNESCO Assistant Director in the Department of Education, Paris; Leo Fernig had responded positively and had promised sympathetic support to ISA to carry out such a pilot project (Leach 1991). A parallel event occurred at the UNESCO General Conference of 1962 when the United Arabic Republic (which comprised Egypt and Yemen at the time) put forward a project to realise a coordinated programme throughout international schools, interchangeable in different countries (Renaud 1974, p6-7). This was thanks to Asme Nawar, a teacher at the International School of Geneva and friend of Cole-Baker and Leach, who had approached his Egyptian compatriots and persuaded them of the merit of the IB project. This motion assisted further funding by UNESCO to ISA in April 1963 for 'Co-ordination of Academic Standards and Curricula Among International Schools'. The support from UNESCO provided approval of the direction in which the ISA was moving with regard to an international diploma. These were also contributing factors that assisted ISA's decision to move ahead.

Contemporary history course – 1963
The history department at the International School of Geneva under Leach's direction, ably assisted by Michael Knight, Eugene Wallach, Phil Thomas and others, set about responding immediately to ISA's recommendation of September 1962 with the full support of Cole-Baker and John Goormaghtigh, chair of the school board. This pilot project was the precursor to a full international curriculum and examination. Initial funding came from both ISA and the International School of Geneva (Cole-Baker 1992) after the UNESCO grant to ISA of US$2500 for the Conference of Teachers of Social Studies in International Schools. Leach was a prime force for enthusing the teachers, and the executive committee of ISA, in their quest for an international contemporary history syllabus and for the development of a whole series of subjects in the same vein.

By February 1963, Leach and his group of teachers, with assistance from UNIS, had completed the international contemporary history syllabus and examination, which was printed by UNESCO under a 'Mutual Appreciation of Eastern and Western Cultures' contract with ISA. This was sent to many ministries and departments of education throughout the world and 40 encouraging responses were received (Hayot 1984, p232).

In June 1963 five students of the International School of Geneva took the contemporary history exam, which was a move away from encyclopaedic knowledge – the hallmark of equivalent national exams in the UK, France and western Germany – towards a more reflective, analytical approach. One of these students was accepted by Harvard (Leach 1969a, p48). This exam was then taken 'regularly each year until 1971 when the full roster of IB exams was sat' (Leach 1991a). The students who voluntarily presented themselves for this examination still had to sit their appropriate national history papers. However, Leach had no trouble finding willing candidates.

History was chosen as the starting point for an international programme because it was recognised as a subject particularly prone to national and ideological biases. (This writer remembers attending a meeting at the Council of Europe in Strasbourg in 1994 to discuss a European history course. Several history teachers from central and eastern European countries recounted how they had found themselves, in the immediate wake of recent cultural revolutions, from one day to the next, without suitable textbooks to teach the history of their countries, since those sanctioned by the former political powers no longer had any currency.) The successful development of an international history course would pave the way for other courses less plagued by patriotic interpretations, whether imposed by a government or not. It was not the *content* of the contemporary history course that was to differentiate it from its national counterparts, it was its pedagogical approach. The fundamental premise required students to analyse, explore and appreciate the different interpretations of the same event by various historians operating in diverse cultural contexts. Understanding the complex reasons *why* a particular interpretation exists, without necessarily agreeing with it, gives legitimacy to other points of view; this is the underpinning of an international history course. This should, in turn, lead to mutual respect for other ways of conceiving the world. Such an approach requires critical thinking skills, intercultural understanding, and an awareness of the sources of history and of the potential for bias.

Earlier attempts at such courses had been made – for example, the world history course established at the International School of Geneva by Madame Maurette in the 1930s and 40s. It appears that her course had been consulted during the first developments of the IB history programme, but the *Portrait of*

World History course in three volumes by the English historian and teacher Geoffrey Williams (books I and II were published in 1961 and 1962 respectively) played an important role as Michael Knight (1999, p208), who assisted Leach with the pioneering work, attests: '[*Portrait of World History*] became the mainstay of the groundwork courses leading to the International Baccalaureate Programme in history.'

Other subjects – from 1963
Since the executive of ISA and of the board of the International School of Geneva were composed of many of the same UN civil servants, the impetus that came from the school for further pilot courses was supported by ISA and UNESCO (as a UN agency). So in April 1963 UNESCO awarded a contract to ISA to examine the 'Co-ordination of Academic Standards and Curricula Among International Schools' (Leach 1969b, p80). The UNESCO support was due to the enthusiasm of Leo Fernig.[1] Other courses therefore followed, with major contributions from dedicated teachers at the school such as Gérard Renaud who established philosophy and French language and literature courses; Ruth Bonner and Nansi Poirel worked on German and English language and literature syllabi respectively.

Cole-Baker, an Irishman, was ideologically motivated to extend the successful contemporary history syllabus to other subject areas. He wanted to look at international curricula from primary through to the end of secondary school but saw that the task was too large to tackle at once and decided to concentrate on the last two years of secondary schooling, where problems of university acceptance needed addressing. (In fact, once a structure separate from the ISA had been established for the development of the Diploma Programme, Cole-Baker produced for ISA the first international primary curriculum in 1966.) He asked his teachers whether they believed in international education; when they said 'yes' he urged them to create international syllabi for the two pre-university years. 'Forget everything you have learned; think of the children in the year 2000 and bring me your ideas' he said (Bonner 1990, p41). In a letter of appointment to Phil Thomas, who was engaged to teach geography, Cole-Baker told him that he was to develop a geography programme along the same lines as Leach and his teachers were doing in history (Thomas 1992).

Except for Gérard Renaud and Nan Martin, the teachers of the French section of the school were slow to participate during this initial period from April until the end of October. But in September 1963 an ISA Conference, 'The Teaching of Foreign Languages' held in Milan, explored IB examinations in English *and* French. At this conference three criticisms of language teaching in national education systems were cited: there was:

- an insufficient basis for genuine communication;
- an insufficient link to the study of the life and civilisation of the people who speak the language; and
- too much stress on translation.

International schools provided an ideal setting to overcome these problems, particularly schools with different language groups, such as the International School of Geneva. The IB might become a laboratory for an experimental method of foreign language teaching that could be useful for improving language teaching in national systems. This involved the French section teachers, who then began to participate in the creation of subject syllabi in French and methodological approaches to teaching foreign languages in an international school setting (Peterson 1972, p11).

An ISA examinations advisory committee was established in November 1963, comprising staff of the International School of Geneva and the University of Geneva, to plan IB examination papers for June 1964. (This committee later became the executive committee of the International Schools Examination Syndicate when the latter was created in February 1964). The small grant from UNESCO was quite insufficient to continue the development of a full range of international diploma courses. The enormity of creating, from nothing, a whole international programme of subjects for the last two years of secondary schooling was daunting. Attention had to be given to subject content and how this might be interpreted in different cultural contexts, setting examination papers and having them monitored, obtaining volunteer students to sit an examination with no standing and, of course, funding the research. At this stage, volunteer teachers from the International School of Geneva were developing the subjects of an international diploma in their spare time.

Atlantic College – 1962

Atlantic College opened in September 1962 at St Donat's, Wales, overlooking the Bristol Channel. It became the first of the UWCs. It is a boarding school where, since its inception, approximately 300 students selected for scholarships by national UWC committees in countries around the globe, join together for the last two years of secondary school. It was founded through the inspiration of Kurt Hahn, a German of Jewish origin, who was 'one of the most remarkable educators of his time' (Peterson 1987, p1). He was the founding Headmaster of Salem School (Germany) in 1920. In 1932 he wrote to all former pupils saying they must break with Hitler or break with Salem. He was arrested but escaped to Britain and founded Gordonstoun School in Scotland, which Prince Charles, a former president of the UWC board, later attended. He also founded the

Outward Bound Movement and the Duke of Edinburgh's Award.

These achievements embodied the profound educational and ideological convictions that governed his life. He wanted to change prejudices and the causes of war, and reverse the decline in physical fitness, enterprise, memory and imagination, skill and care, self-discipline and compassion (Peterson 1987, p2). Hahn, with assistance from Sir Lawrance Darvall of NATO, set about establishing Atlantic College. Rear-Admiral Desmond Hoare of the British Navy, an associate of Sir Lawrance Darvall, was appointed as the first Headmaster. A French businessman, Antonin Besse, bought and donated St Donat's Castle; he was chairman of the UWC board for some years and was also very active on the executive committee and council of foundation of the IB organisation.

Alec Peterson was director of the Department of Educational Studies at Oxford University from 1958, having previously been Head of Dover College (UK). He met Hahn at a conference on international education at Bruges (Belgium) organised by NATO and heard about the establishment of Atlantic College. Robert Blackburn (later deputy director-general of the IB until his death in 1990) was appointed deputy headmaster of Atlantic College from his post as head of history in a British school. During the summer of 1962, Peterson worked with him on the curriculum for the new school.

Since students would represent a diverse cultural group, what curriculum should be offered? Peterson had been questioning the narrowness of the three A levels in England. Atlantic College now faced the same problem that the International School of Geneva, Yokohama International School, UNIS and others had experienced: no international university entrance examination was available. The immediate solution was to offer GCE A levels and adopt English as the language of instruction. 'Success in these examinations qualified the students to apply for admission to the university in the seventeen member countries of the Council of Europe under the European Convention on the Equivalence of Diplomas of 1953.' (Peterson 1987, p10) American universities presented no problem, since admission depended on Scholastic Aptitude Tests (SAT) with no prescribed curriculum.

There were, however, a number of difficulties associated with the GCE A level programme in an international school:

1. The 1953 convention guaranteed that the foreign student would not be rejected on the grounds that he/she had a foreign qualification. Students were, however, refused admission where they lacked qualifications in compulsory prerequisite subjects for certain faculties.

2. Most European university entrance examination results appeared in early July while those of the GCE A levels were not available till mid-August, *after* the completion of admission procedures by many European universities.

3. The highly specialised nature of the programme meant that students who had not taken a foreign language or maths could not be admitted to many faculties.

4. The stress on translation from and into English in foreign language examinations disadvantaged all students who did not possess native-like proficiency in English.

5. The examinations were norm-referenced. Grades were therefore awarded with reference to a very large cohort of candidates sitting each year for whom English was the mother tongue. Students for whom English was a foreign language were disadvantaged by this process.

In an effort to overcome these difficulties, Blackburn and Peterson added three 'subsidiary' courses, as opposed to the 'higher' advanced level courses; achievement in the former was recorded on an 'Atlantic College Leaving Certificate'. Students had to complete at least one course from each of the following groups, three at 'higher' and three at 'subsidiary' level:

1. The mother tongue.
2. The first foreign language (usually English for overseas students).
3. A further language or literature course.
4. Social sciences.
5. Maths or sciences.
6. Arts and crafts

In addition, religious instruction, philosophy and current affairs were compulsory (Peterson 1987, p10-13). The similarity between this and the draft proposal for an IB curriculum that was adopted in June 1964 (discussed later) will be obvious, the main difference being that the IB Diploma Programme demanded both maths *and* science.

In 1963 the first graduates were received at a number of European and American universities but the national character of the British examination was not consonant with the educational needs of the international student population. The school adopted the IB exclusively from 1971.

The flurry of curriculum activity by Blackburn and Peterson at Atlantic College occurred at the same time as, but quite independently from, the beginnings of the international contemporary history course at the International School of Geneva by Leach and other staff and the draft proposal for an IB of June 1964. It is remarkable that staff from both schools arrived at such similar ideas since they were not to meet until later in 1964 and Peterson did not have firsthand knowledge of the curriculum development work in Geneva until November 1965.

John Goormaghtigh

John Goormaghtigh, of Belgian nationality, was a parent at the International School of Geneva and Director of the European Office of the Carnegie Endowment for International Peace. In the early 1960s the uneconomical viability of small classes was one factor that influenced him, as chairman of the board, to look for and support an alternative curriculum.

Other board members were also concerned at the effect on tuition fees of the small classes, particularly in the French language section (Goormaghtigh 1991). Goormaghtigh, however, as a result of active service and imprisonment in the concentration camp of Dachau during the Second World War, was not applying only fiscal reasoning to the problem of small class sizes, he was also prompted by ideological concerns about the separation of students into national groups within a school, and believed that a truly international programme and examination could help create a more tolerant world and lead to university entrance across the globe.

Goormaghtigh's influence did not rest on his impressive international status alone. He had a physical presence and assertiveness that people respected. He was a man of 'considerable political vision; an authoritative figure with clout in academic and political circles' (Sutcliffe 1992). This impression is confirmed by others who found him 'intelligent, resourceful, articulate' (Leach 1991), 'an excellent chairman, realistically idealistic' (Gathier 1992), 'a gifted linguist, very practical' (Carus 1992), 'sometimes provocative; he had contacts in the UN and with influential academics and politicians in the USA and Europe' (Bonner 1991). 'He was imposing, confident, had important political connections and understood the need for an IB' (Hanson 1992). Renaud (1991), one of the early architects of the IB and a former director-general of the IB organisation, appropriately summed up Goormaghtigh when he said that he had 'le calibre international'.

The conviction that an IB *must* exist carried the ISA forward; the support of UNESCO and the stature of the ISA members involved, with their important international connections, provided a solid base for officially launching the project. Goormaghtigh, in particular, who saw the IB through its gestation period and for many years after, was a tremendous asset.

Goormaghtigh played a capital role and made the IB politically acceptable. He was a man of international stature and was held in high standing in the city of Geneva. When he gave his imprimatur to the IB idea he automatically brought with him people in the highest educational and political circles in Europe and the United States (Ritchie 1992).

While there were other important international public servants who were directly involved, their presence and support was usually more spasmodic as they came and left Geneva. Goormaghtigh, on the other hand, contributed over a long period. At the time of the ISA recommendation, in August 1962, Goormaghtigh was treasurer of ISA and chairman of the board of the International School of Geneva. His main voluntary activities in relation to international education were:

- treasurer of ISA from 1957-62
- chair of the board of the International School of Geneva 1960-66
- founding president of the IBO council of foundation 1968-81.

He remained very loyal to the IB, regularly attended its council of foundation meetings and gave the inaugural Peterson Lecture in 1989, in memory of Alec Peterson, the first director general of the IB, at the council meeting in Geneva. He died in 1998 at his family home near Strasbourg at 79 years of age.

Notes

1. Leo Fernig started work at UNESCO, Paris, in 1948 and was Assistant Director in education at the time the IB project began. He was Director of UNESCO's International Bureau of Education in Geneva from 1970 until his retirement in 1977, with one year (1974-75) as Acting Assistant Director General for Education in Paris. Fernig introduced the IB to Piet Gathier, Director General of education in the Netherlands (and later president of the IB's council of foundation 1984-90), by inviting him to a council of foundation meeting in 1974. Gathier was on the board of UNESCO's International Bureau of Education in Geneva when Fernig was director (Gathier 1992).

Part IV – The birth of the IB diploma

Introduction

This chapter moves us on from the previous chapter in more or less chronological order, to action taking place in and around 1964-65. In Part III the ISA had recommended (in 1962) that an 'international baccalaureate' of common standards be created and the staff of the International School of Geneva had picked up the challenge. Lacking the infrastructure to undertake curriculum development and student assessment, ISA created the International Schools Examination Syndicate (ISES), discussed in this chapter, which produced a draft profile of an IB Diploma Programme in the middle of 1964.

Subject development meetings began in an organised way from March 1965 when the overall composition of the diploma was firmed up. The creation of the Theory of Knowledge (ToK), from conversations following the March 1965 meeting up to its formal acceptance in 1967, is discussed. The chapter concludes with a sketch of Desmond Cole-Baker, who was very instrumental in enthusing his teachers at the International School of Geneva to get on with developing a programme of international education in which he believed so passionately.

International Schools Examination Syndicate (ISES) – 1964

As initial plans were developing in Geneva it became obvious that here was an undertaking of some magnitude, requiring the creation of a fixed administrative structure with professional educators and a secretariat, together with access to influential international figures. The ISA had existed since 1951 but it was not until February 1964 that the idea of a new organisation, the ISES, was mooted at an ISA meeting to develop the IB exclusively. By June 1964 an ISES structure was in place with a council, an executive committee and a board of examiners. In January 1965, ISES established individual legal identity as an 'association' under the Swiss Civil Code but remained a part of ISA.

At first, all involved with the ISES were unpaid enthusiasts for international education, but it soon became evident that a more formal structure was needed. Ruth Bonner became the first paid employee of ISES in September 1964 as executive secretary (having previously been full-time secretary of the ISA and a teacher at the International School of Geneva before that) but there was still no person to take charge of the project on a daily basis.

In the spring of 1965 the ISES office moved from the pre-fabricated art department building of the International School of Geneva, to a neighbouring villa at 12, chemin de la Chevillarde, about 100 metres from the current central administration building of La Grande Boissière (International School of Geneva).

Knowledge about the curriculum work taking place in Geneva reached Peterson via Bill Halls, a lecturer in education at Oxford involved in comparative education research. Halls was also a French language scholar and colleague of Recteur Capelle, a reformer of the French *baccalauréat* who joined the ISES council from 1966. The International School of Geneva was one of the institutions to which the Oxford Department of Educational Studies had been sending teacher trainees. Halls heard about the IB project and informed Peterson, who attended his first ISES council meeting on the 4th November 1965 in Geneva (Peterson 1965). That was the beginning of his long and fruitful involvement with the IB.

In November 1965 Peterson and Goormaghtigh were in communication about the appointment of Dr Bill Halls as director of ISES; Peterson agreed to an initial period of release from Oxford for the 1966-67 academic year. This did not eventuate but he later became director of the IB Oxford Research Unit. Peterson himself was appointed part-time director from July 1966 and full-time from January 1967, when he moved to Geneva for six months during his sabbatical from Oxford.

ISES was created through an agreement between ISA and the International School of Geneva to develop a common programme and university admission examinations for the last two years of secondary school. The founding of ISES was the result of a recommendation to Cole-Baker from the staff in his school who wanted a structure to administer the work in which they were becoming deeply involved. Cole-Baker agreed, although somewhat reluctantly; he would have preferred that the ISA be strengthened and expanded to take on many aspects of international education, including the IB (Cole-Baker 1989). 'If ISA had had the structure it should have had, ISES would not have been necessary.' (Ritchie 1992) This is also a reference to the preponderance of international civil servants giving voluntarily of their time to ISA. Professional educators employed full-time would be needed to launch the IB. Indeed, the ISA did not have the structure to continue with such a large project as well as providing assistance in other ways to international schools. It was left to concentrate on primary and middle school curricula, two of the four originating schools of ISA being nursery schools (Leach 1969a, p24).

ISES consisted of a council, administration committee, examinations board and an executive committee. Goormaghtigh eventually relinquished his chairmanship of the board of the International School of Geneva and his membership of the executive of ISA to become chair of the first, 11-member, council.[1]

Cole-Baker was the only school representative on the council; all other members were university staff or employed by international organizations. This was necessary because the ISES was to ensure the credibility and appropriate standard of the IB exams leading to university entrance. Robert Blackburn of Atlantic College (Wales) later joined the ISES council; his school was the most active promoter of the IB after the International School of Geneva (Leach 1969a, p42) together with UNIS, New York.

The administration committee was headed by Cole-Baker with three council members. One of their main tasks was to check the qualifications of the members of the examinations board.

The examinations board of six comprised all university academics from Geneva with the exception of one person from the USA. This board was responsible for the conduct of the examinations – in particular the setting of papers and the appointment of examiners.[2]

The executive committee comprised mostly teachers from the International School of Geneva. The president was E Wallach, deputy head of the department of history, with Bob Leach as secretary and Cole-Baker a member. This committee concentrated on curriculum development and worked with the examinations board in the preparation of examinations. It was very much a technical, not an administrative, committee. This group was involved very much in action research, whereby curriculum ideas were introduced in the classroom and amended in the light of this practical experience.

So, although the title implied an interest only in examinations, from the inception of the ISES a curriculum development committee existed. This group of actors were mostly university staff who were brought officially into the IB project for the first time. The council of the ISES soon attracted major reformers in national education systems: for example, Peterson (UK), Madame Hatinguais and Recteur Capelle (French ministry of education), Hellmut Becker of the Max Planck Institute and Heinz Fischer-Wolpert from Germany. For these and others the IB project corresponded to their own ideals concerning educational objectives, content, methodology, student assessment practices and academic requirements. Here was an educational laboratory that offered exciting solutions to pedagogical problems. The quality of educational discussion across cultures was of an exceptionally high order; it provided the best possible underpinning for the IB Diploma Programme, which is still standing the test of time.

The setting and correction of examinations was carried out by examiners who were initially university academics of standing in their own countries; this was essential to ensure acceptance of the IB by universities. As time went on, experienced IB teachers also became examiners, though even today the chief examiners are largely university staff. It is noteworthy that the curriculum development aspect was the province of teachers (at the International School of Geneva initially). This enhanced the acceptability of the programme: teachers in schools contemplating the introduction of the IB had faith in their colleagues who were closest to the needs of the international student. The teachers' interest in the IB stemmed from their belief in intercultural understanding and an education that would provide access to any university for the internationally mobile student.

An 'ISES Day' was held at the International School of Geneva on 19 May 1964 at which some French section staff were also present. This was the first formal gathering to explore the creation of international syllabi and examinations across a range of subjects; informal work, at Cole-Baker's instigation, had already occurred in English, French and philosophy. An 'Introductory Session for Teaching Staff' was given by Cole-Baker, Goormaghtigh and Siotis, a professor at the University of Geneva and president of the ISES examinations committee. During the rest of the morning and afternoon, groups formed to discuss a schema for each of the following disciplines: languages, sciences, mathematics, fine arts and social studies. Cole-Baker provided the following advice to the staff:

1. Imagine you have the ideal syllabus.
2. Jot down a detailed outline on a piece of paper.
3. Exploit the international environment in which international schools are located.

(ISES 1964).

Draft proposal for an international baccalaureate – June 1964

In June 1964 a document was published in the *ISA Newsletter Bulletin* entitled 'Draft Proposal for an International Baccalaureate'. The ISA social studies conference of 1962 is described as the catalyst for the contemporary history examination, which then spread to other subjects and to the creation of the ISES in February 1964. The document emanates from the staff of the International School of Geneva; it provides a succinct rationale for an IB and suggestions about the subject profile of the diploma.

A more general educational background covering man's achievements on an international scale was seen as preferable to over-specialisation within the confines of one national heritage and culture (a clear reference to English A levels). Literature and philosophy of different cultures was important for the international student; hence world literature and philosophy courses should be compulsory. (World literature, as part of the first language, and the ToK are both obligatory subject requirements today).

It was suggested that the examination be offered at two levels. Firstly as a lower level certificate at the end of the second or third last year of secondary school, for those not contemplating tertiary education, and then as a higher level university entrance examination after seven years of secondary schooling. The lower level examination would require three subjects: a first language, a second language and mathematics. For the higher level examination five more subjects should be taken from:

1. chemistry, physics, biology; and
2. history, geography, art, music, a third language.

At least two subjects were to be chosen from each of groups 1 and 2.

An eight-subject university entrance examination was, then, proposed. The subject categories of this first proposal by staff of the International School of Geneva have been virtually maintained by the IB diploma to the present. The variation is that the second group above became two of the current six subject divisions with other disciplines added:

• Group 3: history, geography, economics, philosophy, psychology.
• Group 6: art, music, third language, theatre.

This draft document provided the basis for many subsequent discussions until the end of the 1960s on syllabus and examination content, and the structure of the diploma.

In October 1964 Atlantic College invited teachers from the International School of Geneva to Wales to discuss the origins and objectives of the IB, its structure and official languages, and syllabus construction. Wallach (science), Poirel (English), Howenstine (mathematics) and Renaud (French and philosophy) from the International School of Geneva met with Rear-Admiral Desmond Hoare, the Headmaster, and 13 other teachers of Atlantic College. It was at this meeting that the idea of higher and subsidiary level subjects was first raised, based on the Atlantic College model. This was the beginning of the involvement of Atlantic College in the IB project.

Curriculum development meetings – from 1965

March 11-15, 1965, saw the first IB curriculum study conference in Geneva to discuss the overall configuration of the IB; the six major discipline areas were established. Five subject committees sat, each chaired by a teacher of the International School of Geneva: history (Leach), biology (Unitt), maths (Mrs Howenstine), geography (Thomas) and modern languages (Madame Martin). The universities of Geneva, Lausanne, Sussex, Birmingham, Manchester and London, CERN (European Nuclear Research Centre, Geneva), Atlantic College and the French ministry of education had representatives in one or more subject committees. There were some 40 participants, including Martin Mayer of the Twentieth Century Fund who was there to check on progress, and to gather material for a book he was writing on the IB project linked to a grant from that fund, which had been approved in principle in December 1964. When, prior to this event, Cole-Baker had reported that this curriculum study conference was about to take place, the board of the International School of Geneva noted with interest that it had attracted educators from a number of countries (International School of Geneva Board Minutes, 9th March 1965). The link between the international school, ISA and ISES was strong.

André Van Smeevoorde, the French ministry representative, was the chief inspector for languages. There was quite a discussion about the profile of the Diploma Programme, particularly concerning the extent to which students should be able to choose subjects: it was principally an English/French debate whereby George Bruce of the London GCE board wanted a quite liberal choice while Van Smeevoorde wanted virtually no choice. To overcome the impasse, Renaud spent a late night session with Van Smeevoorde and they arrived at a compromise that Renaud presented on the blackboard the next morning. It was that no individual subject, except two languages and mathematics, would be specified and students must then choose at least one subject from each of the following groups: humanities, laboratory science, and an arts and electives group. Renaud can claim to have been the architect of this basic profile, which has not changed since (Peterson 1987, p28-29). On his return to Paris after the conference, Van Smeevoorde gained the collaboration of one of his colleagues, Tric, who agreed to be examiner for philosophy and was instrumental in the creation of the ToK.

The second curriculum study conference occurred in October 1965 at Atlantic College to discuss languages. Three *inspecteurs généraux* from the French ministry of education were also present: Van Smevoorde for English, Morisset for French and Holderith for German.

During the first ISES executive committee meeting after the March 1965 IB curriculum study conference, Mayer urged ISES to proceed with the development of syllabi and examination papers. He was impressed with the whole idea but he was to have some reservations about the organisation and the administration of ISES to take on such a large task. The ISES executive now had two major roles: marketing the IB and 'shepherding its educational development' (Leach 1969a, p59).

What we now know as 'creativity, action, service' (CAS) and the extended essay were not there in 1965; they were to come later.

The Theory of Knowledge (ToK)

Monsieur Tric, an *inspecteur général* from the education ministry in Paris, had agreed to elaborate a philosophy curriculum as a humanities option. Some months after the March 1965 meeting in Paris, Gérard Renaud was talking with Tric who regretted that philosophy was not compulsory (as it is in the French *baccalauréat*). Renaud shared his concern but was also aware that in the Anglo-Saxon world philosophy was seen essentially as a study of metaphysics, doctrines, and so on – something for specialists in higher education and not appropriate at the school level. They discussed this problem and arrived at the idea of including an element of reflection in the IB programme that would not be called 'philosophy' and which would not be examined. Renaud (1986, p7) remarks:

> At a certain moment – I can no longer remember exactly how – there was mention of a theory of knowledge course which would not cover the whole field of philosophy but an essential aspect of it. The idea had been found. It remained to have it accepted by the others.

The idea was mooted, discussed and officially accepted at the Sèvres curriculum conference in 1967, where we read in the minutes of Commissions A & B chaired by Peterson (IB Conference, Sèvres 1967):

> That the Theory of Knowledge course should not be examined but teachers of this course should submit a report on their students to the Examining Board. Such reports would allow a fuller understanding of the candidates and could be of considerable help in border-line cases.

By 1970 teachers were asked to assess students in ToK on a seven point scale like the other diploma subjects. A score of six or seven would add one more point to the total number of diploma points while a score of one or two in this subject would cause one point to be deducted from the total. The chief examiner for philosophy acted as moderator for ToK and could, and did, call for samples of work. In Commission A, chaired by Fischer-Wollpert, two new elements of the IB were discussed: world literature and the ToK. The latter was 'accepted by most participants as one of the most important features in the IB'. Peterson took a great interest in the course and became involved in its development, as did Andrew Maclehose, one of the original teachers at Atlantic College.

So a compromise had been reached whereby philosophy remained an option in the humanities group of subjects but all students must follow a course in ToK, a course that explored, *inter alia*, the connections between the different branches of knowledge and encouraged students to reflect critically on their experiences. This provided a unifying, reflective and trans-disciplinary subject that is today regarded as the cornerstone of the IB Diploma Programme.

The first ToK syllabus was produced in French by Madame Dina Dreyfus of the French ministry of education for the 1970 IB general guide, and refined by her for the 1972 guide. She produced, at the same time, a teacher's guide with pedagogical ideas for the classroom. Madame Dreyfus had replaced Tric in the curriculum development meetings and became chief examiner for philosophy from 1969 until 1979. She and Georges Laforest (from 1980), both *inspecteurs généraux* in Paris, were the principal moderators of student peformance in ToK (and philosophy) for many years. Sue Bastian of the UNIS, New York, also became one of the developers and assessors who maintained a long association with the subject.

Desmond Cole-Baker

Cole-Baker had been drawn into teaching in international schools because of active service during the Second World War in the British Corps of Signals in Africa, Sri Lanka, India and Burma. After the war he returned to his native Ireland and underwent training as a teacher. In 1955 he was appointed head of the science department at the International School of Geneva and made responsible for secondary school curriculum. He immediately became interested in the ISA and its consultative mission towards international schools. Influenced by Roquette, who was the Head of the school, Cole-Baker also talked about the need for an international university entrance qualification. In 1961 he became head of the English language section, and Head of the whole school in 1964 when Roquette retired after 33 years of service. He prepared the submission that led to the successful Ford Foundation grant for the development of the IB project and went to New York to meet with officials of the foundation in 1964.

One international curriculum and examination offered in English and French was appealing to Cole-Baker because he saw it as a means of merging the English and French sections of the school, thus producing even more viable class groups and a true bilingual context where students would have some of their subjects in each language. Following lengthy debate he decided to go ahead. The proposed dismissal of superfluous teachers did, however, cause major resentment amongst the staff and a rift in the governing board and parent organisation. Therefore the two sections were not amalgamated and continued to offer a French baccalaureate and the Swiss *maturité* in the French section, the IB being offered in the English section. This was a major crisis in the history of the school and it damaged Cole-Baker's reputation. He resigned in 1968, very disappointed, but continued for three years as secretary of the ISA.

He had wanted ISA to create its own infrastructure to develop the IB Diploma Programme and to consider international education programmes for all school ages, not just the last two years of secondary school. He left the ISA in 1971.

What I had really wanted to do was to create an independent

international education authority, which could consider education worldwide, without political strictures. I felt that there could be a great deal of useful exchange of views and material between such an organisation and governments. The IB would have been part of this organisation and not a separate body. I could not get enough people to think on this scale (Cole-Baker 1989).

He was a fervent supporter of the ideology of promoting world peace through international understanding and saw the mixing of cultural groups in schools as a step towards this goal (Cole-Baker 1989). He was also a forceful character – convincing and idealistic: 'He had an excellent reputation as a leader in education.' (Bonner 1991). 'He ruled the staff with an iron hand and enthused with his missionary zeal.' (Thomas 1992). 'He caught you up in his enthusiasm; he had vision and courage.' (Poirel 1991). Gellar (1991) commented: 'He was the kindest man in the world.'

Elisabeth Briquette pays tribute to him in the following terms:

I think he was the most popular teacher the English Language Program has ever known. Popular, not only because of his geniality and efficiency, but by reason of this heartfelt, almost fanatical belief in the clear duty of the International School of Geneva to lead the international schools of the world, springing up year after year in Asia, Europe, Africa, America, destined to help lead, as he hoped, quarrelling humanity into the path of peace. (*Ecole Internationale de Genève: 50e Anniversaire 1924-1974.* 1974, p225).

He visited Geneva in April 1999 from his home in New Zealand. It was then that I met him for the first time at a lunch given in his honour at the International School of Geneva. I had corresponded with him some years before, about his involvement in the launching of the IB diploma. His vision in the 1960s of three international programmes for children from three to 19 years of age had finally been realised in 1997 when the IB organization adopted the last of the three: the Primary Years Programme (PYP). Cole-Baker was enthusiastic about this. He had lost none of his forcefulness and was pleased to see some of the staff he had worked with more than 30 years before. He was given the ISA Distinguished Service Award for international education in February 2000.

Notes

1. First ISES council, February 1964. (Hill 1994, p389)

President	J Goormaghtigh	Director, European Office of the Carnegie Endowment for International Peace, Geneva
Vice-President	J Freymond	Director of the University Institute of Higher International Studies, Switzerland
Secretary	E Kozera	Administrative Secretary of the International Commission of Jurists, USA
Treasurer	D Cole-Baker	Headmaster of the International School of Geneva
Members	P Chu (China)	Advisor in the Division of Education for Workers at the International Labour Office, Geneva
	M Sarwate (India)	Assistant Secretary General of the Union of International Workers
	G Hampton (UK)	Director of CERN (Centre Européen de Recherche Nucléaire - the European Nuclear Research Centre)
	G Panchaud (Switzerland)	Professor of Pedagogy at the University of Lausanne
	D Davies (UK)	Secretary General of the World Health Organisation
	Madame H Marquand (France)	Director of the International Institute of Social Studies
	C Bonner (UK)	Curator of the Botanical Collection of Cryptogams in Geneva

2. First ISES examinations board 1964. (Hill 1994, p389-90)

President	J Siotis (Greece)	Professor of the Graduate Institute of International Studies and Lecturer in International Law at the University of Geneva
Members	H Kapur (India)	Lecturer at the University of Geneva
	A Overstreet (USA)	Professor of Political Sciences, Smith College
	Madame H Pfaendler (Switzerland)	Lecturer in Foreign Languages at the University of Geneva
	D Janjic (Yugoslavia)	Lecturer in Chemistry at the University of Geneva
	M Stroun (Switzerland)	Lecturer in Genetics at the University of Geneva

Part V – The ISA primary curriculum and early donors to the IB project

Introduction

Parts III and IV described the beginnings of the IB Diploma Programme at the International School of Geneva in the early 1960s, with the development of the first history syllabus by Robert Leach and the encouragement from Desmond Cole-Baker, head of the English language section, to develop other IB subjects.

This chapter commences with a brief description of the little-known ISA international primary curriculum and its link with Cole-Baker. It then turns to the important contributions of UNESCO, the Twentieth Century Fund (now known as the Century Fund) and the Ford Foundation to the continuing development of the IB Diploma Programme project during the 1960s and beyond.

An ISA international primary school curriculum – 1966

In a letter to me in 1989 Desmond Cole-Baker (see Part IV) of the International School of Geneva had indicated that he wanted the ISA to undertake international education from K-12:

> I set about tackling three matters: an international Primary School Curriculum, an international Leaving Certificate ... and giving assistance in forming or reorganising schools in mainly developing countries. You will notice that the middle school was left out for the moment but I had to set priorities. (Cole-Baker 1989)

The international leaving certificate became the IB Diploma Programme. As for the primary project, teachers from international schools met in their spare time in different institutions and, as the project developed, certain schools were given the task of preparing a specific part of the programme. *An International Primary School Curriculum ISA*, compiled and edited by Cole-Baker, was first published in 1966 and revised in 1970. It was not widely distributed and few copies remain today. (The International Schools Curriculum Project group of the early 1990s, supported by the European Council of International Schools (ECIS) and also the IB organization, was not aware of the existence of the 1966 document when they launched the international primary programme that was to become the IB's PYP in 1997.)

The ISA/Cole-Baker publication represents guidelines (with suggested content) for 'internationally standardised curricula' rather than placing emphasis on an international perspective. This may have been deliberate, given that governments at the time would not have supported an international perspective but would have been attracted to setting standards for education worldwide.

Seven subject areas are identified: the language of instruction, mathematics, environmental studies, science, language teaching, creative activities (art and music), and physical education. Social studies (history and geography) are integrated to some extent into the science and environmental studies subjects and do not stand alone. 'Foreign language teaching' is considered as one of the primary tasks of an international primary school from a very early age, particularly to learn the language of the host country. Reference to the new methods of the day – direct (using the language all the time in the classroom), and audio lingual – are made with an emphasis on being able to speak in real life situations. Physical education is the only subject in which student evaluation is addressed in some detail. Maths is to rely on the *discovery* method: moving from concrete situations to general rules.

Much stress is placed on using new teaching methods of the time, and on teaching *how* to learn. The teacher is described as a catalyst, adviser, facilitator, not the dispenser of knowledge; he/she should be approachable, broad-minded and have faith in children. Working cooperatively, adaptability and relating to the real world are stated aims of the programme.

The content of the 192 page book is uneven: 100 pages is given to the science course (perhaps reflecting the fact that Cole-Baker was a science teacher), 20 pages to mathematics, and a few pages to the rest. An emphasis on inquiry learning in the science, mathematics and environmental studies programmes provides a link with the current PYP: 'Children's questions are extremely important: the child's own question is the most significant for him and has the most motivating power.' (Cole-Baker 1970, p51) A hint of the PYP's holistic, trans-disciplinary approach appears as part of scientific inquiry, which should lead back into mathematics, language, and other areas '... and this is truly the world of the child who sees the world as a whole and not in terms of subjects' (Cole-Baker 1970, p161).

It is in the science pages that Cole-Baker's philosophy of education becomes apparent. There is emphasis on developing skills and attitudes, and exploiting the natural curiosity of children. Content is not regarded as the most important curriculum element.

We should not worry about the *content* [author's italics] of what is learnt, not because we do not think it is important, but because we believe that it is secondary to the attitude of mind. And experience shows us that, given the chance to range freely, children will venture into all the traditional areas of science. The coverage is there without our having to engineer it. (Cole-Baker 1970, p161).

The words 'intercultural understanding' occur rarely in the book. One example is in reference to Africans and Europeans having different notions of 'our town' and 'animal life' (Cole-Baker 1970, p162). Nevertheless it represents a sound, enlightened pedagogical approach in tune with much of current PYP practice and somewhat ahead of its time for the 1960s. It was not widely used and was quickly forgotten, probably because the driving force, Cole-Baker, left the International School of Geneva in 1968 and the ISA in 1971.

Initial funding

Without financial assistance to pay salaries and travel, to set up an office and to supply materials, the IB project would not have proceeded. The Twentieth Century Fund and the Ford Foundation gave the most support. Other benevolent foundations gave assistance at a later stage. The Ford Foundation funding was the most substantial. UNESCO provided a number of small contracts to ISA, and later to the IB office; while individually small, these contracts provided considerable assistance over time.

UNESCO – 1960s and 1970s

UNESCO's numerous small grants were almost exclusively for curriculum development and student assessment. At the August 1964 ISA general assembly in Paris, UNESCO showed its support for ISES as part of ISA and stated that all contracts would be negotiated with ISA. They were later granted directly to IB. UNESCO's contribution and moral support were of immense value, particularly during the early days when an international university entrance diploma was but a gleam in the eye of a few visionaries.

Some UNESCO projects were particularly associated with the idea of devising an international university-entrance diploma and led to grants such as the following:

- A US$2500 grant to ISA for the Conference of Teachers of Social Studies in International Schools held at the International School of Geneva in 1962, which resulted in the trialling of a contemporary history examination for international schools.

- A grant to ISA for the 'Coordination of Academic Standards and Curricula Among International Schools', which assisted curriculum development in other areas. (April 1963)

- A grant to ISA in 1964 under a UNESCO project concerning the exchange of eastern and western cultural material between international schools (Leach 1969, p50).

- A 1968 contract with ISA to study the comparability of university-entrance examinations (IB 1968, p1).

The figure for the last three grants above was approximately US$2000 each. In October 1964 UNESCO Circular Number 8 *International Understanding at School* appeared; this was a circular pertaining to the UNESCO Associated Schools Project under Education for International Understanding. A large part of the circular was devoted to 'A Study of the Problem of Coordinating Academic Standards and Curricula Among International Schools'; it was a report on progress resulting from the April 1963 UNESCO grant to ISA mentioned above. This funding enabled the curriculum study committee of ISA to prepare a report on the standardisation of curricula together with outline syllabi for social studies, mathematics and art. 'Much of the re-orientation of the syllabus has been done in the Associated Schools Project.' (UNESCO 1964, p3). UNESCO's Associated Schools Project created a network of schools across the world, and particularly in developing countries, whereby ideas and materials were exchanged and links forged to the mutual advantage of the schools; it is still actively functioning today. This is one of a number of examples of indirect financial support to the IB project by UNESCO using its own communication links to promulgate the IB programme to schools involved in the Associated Schools Project.

The circular concluded with the findings of the ISA curriculum study committee, which favoured a standardised core curriculum with adaptations to local conditions. This standardised curriculum should lead to the establishment of 'an international baccalaureate or matriculation examination'. The examination should provide 'an internationally valid scale for evaluating students' achievements; it could help solve the delicate problem of equivalence, and might eventually bring about more flexibility in national examination systems' (UNESCO 1964, p9).

From 1974 to 1979 UNESCO granted nine contracts to the IB office totalling US$36,000. These contracts were to undertake research associated with approved UNESCO programmes that happened to aid IB curriculum design. The purpose and amount of each contract is listed below in Table 1. The duration of each project was from six to 12 months.

Purpose	Date begun	Amount $US
Follow-up study of IB graduates and evaluation of ToK course	18.4.74	$10,000
Evaluation of testing and assessment in the IB	28.5.75	$10,000
Nutritional sciences curriculum	9.5.77	$2000
Articulation of IB objectives with university education	18.10.77	$2000
Evaluation of moral education in selected IB schools	25.10.77	$1500
Development of assessment procedures	15.11.77	$2000
Comparative study of proposed IB maths programme for non-mathematicians	17.11.77	$2000
Educational needs of the internationally-mobile student	24.8.78	$4000
Organisation of international maths conference in Sèvres, 19-23 March 1979, to review existing syllabi and discuss proposed 'maths & computing' and 'computer studies' courses	14.2.79	$2500
	Total	$36,000

Table 1: UNESCO contracts with the IB office 1974 to 1979. (From IBO File: UNESCO Contracts with IB Office)

The UNESCO contribution was, then, an important continuing support that advanced the development of the IB through research into the needs of internationally displaced students, the adequacy of preparation for university, the construction and reception of specific courses, assessment procedures, and the extent to which the IB programme had been able to form desirable attitudes (moral education). Leach's initial contact with Leo Fernig, who was later Assistant Director-General for Education at UNESCO, Paris, had roused the latter's interest in the IB, which he maintained throughout his career.

UNESCO's support was related to the educational challenge of devising curricula from a multicultural perspective, which would promote intercultural understanding. This was all undertaken against the political backdrop concerning world peace and cooperation. Education officers of UNESCO were satisfied after their technical analysis of curriculum development reports and continued to offer small contracts to assist this work.

The Twentieth Century Fund (now the Century Fund) – 1965 and 1968

After the ISA general assembly of 1962, that association submitted a research project proposal to the Twentieth Century Fund. Finance was sought for the creation of a series of international examinations starting with contemporary history and assessing reactions in different parts of the world. The research would:

- assess actual conditions in international schools;
- evaluate work on standardised curricula;
- investigate the possibility of international syllabi; and
- assess reaction in various countries to an international examination and its acceptance for university entrance.

The project should lead to the publication of a book; hence a first-rate author should accompany the research team. A full-time secretariat and a team of teachers were needed. The team, with the author, would visit groups of countries to allow practical assessment of the need for such an international examination. The budget forecast was for US$75,000 (ISA 1962a).

Leach made contact with Georges-Henri Martin (a Swiss national), member of the board of the International School of Geneva and editor of the *Tribune de Genève* newspaper (Leach 1991a and Cole-Baker 1992). Martin recalls receiving a visit from Leach to discuss a common history programme for international schools and the preparation of the ISA funding proposal (written largely by Leach) to the Twentieth Century Fund (IB 1990, p15). Martin, a former foreign correspondent in Washington for French and Swiss newspapers, had two boys at the International School of Geneva. He was very influential, with important links to the USA. (Before retirement he was president of the academic council of the University of Geneva). His enthusiasm secured the first major financial support for the IB project (Peterson 1972, preface). As a trustee of the Twentieth Century Fund, Martin arranged for August Heckscher, the director, to meet with a committee from the International School of Geneva in the autumn of 1964 to discuss the IB proposal. Heckscher was President Kennedy's adviser on the arts.

Heckscher, after visiting Geneva in September 1964 and speaking with Cole-Baker, Goormaghtigh and others, sent Martin Mayer to Geneva from the 26th to the 28th of November of the same year. Mayer, a professional educator, had been a consultant to the American Council of Learned Societies and a member of the President's Panel on Educational Research. He had published three books on education and was research director for the Twentieth Century Fund (*Twentieth Century Fund Annual Report* 1965, p38).

Mayer reported that the IB proposal was fascinating but that the organisation was very weak and needed considerable financial support to strengthen it

(Mayer 1968, p4). On the 8th of December 1964, Cole-Baker received a letter from Heckscher saying that the Twentieth Century Fund had agreed in principle to grant US$75,000 to the ISES in instalments over the next three years – 1965 to 1968. The Fund commissioned Martin Mayer to write a book on the project and to work with ISES to establish a detailed budget for the use of these funds. The funding proposal as originally presented by the ISA was, then, accepted. The grant was for 'administrative costs, travel, and conferences and workshops' (Twentieth Century Fund 1990). The Twentieth Century Fund responded because its representatives were influenced by actors of high leverage such as Georges-Henri Martin of the *Tribune de Genève* and they saw the educational potential that technical analysis of the programme had thus far revealed.

In 1968 the Twentieth Century Fund gave a further grant of US$75,000 for three more years. 'Although this did allow us to extend our curriculum studies and to employ some permanent staff, we still needed a much more substantial income to get the project off the ground.' (Cole-Baker 1989) The Ford Foundation then proved to be a major benefactor.

The Ford Foundation – 1966 and 1968

The reader will remember that the Ford Foundation had already demonstrated an interest in international education with its grant of US$85,000 to UNIS in 1955 to develop international primary school curricula and to study the application in the USA of the UNIS experience in international education (ISA 1955). In August 1963, Knight (of the International School of Geneva) unsuccessfully visited the Ford Foundation in New York 'on behalf of the embryonic ISES to promote the IB idea and seek funding' (Knight 1992).

In March and April 1964 an ISES mission went to the USA to introduce the IB. Leach and Siotis had sent letters to the Carnegie, Ford and Rockefeller foundations and followed this up with a visit from the 1st to the 15th of April 1964. They spent the 9th and 10th of April at the offices of the Ford Foundation. There was interest, and the Ford Foundation said they would visit Geneva with a consultant. This foundation was investing several million US dollars in providing a new building for UNIS and thought that the new curriculum development emanating from Geneva would suit the school (Peterson 1987, p22).

During June and July of 1965, Cole-Baker persuaded the board of the International School of Geneva to send 16 teachers to an education conference in Denver, Colorado. 'Members went in pairs on different routes in Canada and the USA, some going a few weeks before the conference, others after the meeting.' (Cole-Baker 1990 p38) The visit had two objectives: to broaden the pedagogical and curriculum outlook of the teaching staff and to inform schools and universities of IB developments in Geneva.

The Ford Foundation consultant did go to Geneva in June 1965 and spoke with Cole-Baker (who had not joined the 16 staff in North America). Cole-Baker gave him details of the IB programme.

[The consultant] considered the project worthy of consideration and advised me that the Ford Foundation would be meeting in a few weeks to make grants for the coming year. ... My secretary and I worked virtually non-stop for three days to put together the facts and the future developments. I received a letter from the Ford Foundation asking me to attend a lunch in New York to put forward the case. A reception was also arranged for the evening in order that a number of interested people might question me on the project (Cole-Baker 1990, p38-39).

Cole-Baker went to New York and asked Nansi Poirel and Gérard Renaud (who were part of the Geneva staff visiting Canada and the USA) to join him at the evening reception and give their views.

Although interested, the Ford Foundation had some doubts about the capacity of the ISES and the teachers at the school in Geneva to be able to undertake such a huge project. Firm and credible leadership was needed. In a report to the Twentieth Century Fund, Mayer described some of the reasons that may have contributed to the uneasiness felt by the Ford Foundation:

From mid-1965 to mid-1966, ISES staggered through a series of personal crises, questionable financial allocations and unsatisfactory panel meetings, while the Council resisted any expansion of the membership which would diminish the influence of Geneva (Mayer 1968, p225).

Leach reports that ISES was almost without funds at that time (Leach 1969a, p61). Peterson, of unquestionable educational stature and with diplomatic connections, agreed to become part-time director of ISES. Together with Harlan Hanson (director, Advanced Placement Programme, College Entrance Examination Board, USA, 1965-99, and member of the first IB council of foundation in 1967) they met for one hour with Shep Stone in the New York offices of the Ford Foundation in late 1966. The preliminary overtures dating back to Knight in 1963 had ensured that the IB project was well known. Peterson and Hanson gave the reassurance that the Ford Foundation needed and a solid commitment by Oxford and the College Entrance Examination Board (CEEB) respectively (Peterson 1987, p23).

They were successful, as the following extract from the 'International Understanding' section of the Ford Foundation Annual Report 1966 shows.

One problem of international education is the wide difference in college entrance requirements in various countries, which often makes it difficult for a high-school graduate in one country to qualify for a university in another. For this reason, the Foundation made a grant of US$300,000 to the International Schools Examination Syndicate, in Geneva, for design of an international examination; a student who passed it would be entitled to enter most of the world's colleges and universities. Funds will also be used to improve the examination through consultation with national experts, negotiate its acceptance, and establish standards for grading it (*Ford Foundation Annual Report* 1966, p34).

This quotation provides evidence of factors that influenced the Foundation to grant the money. Obviously its representatives were attracted to the idea of a project that would alleviate difficulties of access to universities, but they were also attracted by the educational potential of the IB programme as a result of technical analysis. This is not to say that they were uninterested in the ideological and cultural aspects, but the pedagogical spin-off for national American schools loomed large in their decision to support the project. In addition Shep Stone was impressed by the high educational leverage of Peterson and Hanson who represented two of the most prestigious universities in the world – Oxford and Harvard (Hanson had a Harvard PhD and had lectured there) – and who held highly influential positions.

The grant was for three years and was made in October 1966. Cole-Baker saw the clinching of this grant as the turning point of the exercise. 'With these funds we were able to enlarge the whole operation to cover the entire spectrum of subjects and employ a complete secretariat.' (Cole-Baker 1992) Moreover, the awarding of the Ford Foundation grant meant that UNIS would be more involved in the IB project. Forward planning was now able to proceed.

The continuation of the Ford Foundation grant depended on raising other funds, which the Foundation would match. During the 1967 and 1968 school year benefactors included the following:

Benefactor	Amount	Frequency
UK Department of Education and Science	£4800	per year for four years
Dulverton Trust	£12,000	per year for six years
Calouste Gulbenkian Fund	US$12,000	per year for three years
Wenner Gren Foundation	US$6000	per year for three years
Twentieth Century Fund	US$25,000	per year for three years
UNESCO	US$2000	

(ISA 1968b).

To these should be added grants from the Netherlands Government, the Federal German Government, and some contributions from banks and industrial corporations (Peterson 1972, p31). In 1969 Mountbatten secured an audience for Peterson with the Shah of Iran, which resulted in a grant of US$100,000 to IB. Blouke Carus, who soon became a council member, negotiated US$20,000 from the Hegeler Institute in the USA in 1974-75 (Peterson 1987, p90), which helped the establishment of the IB North American office (IBNA). Shortly after, Hanson secured funding up to a total of US$330,000 from the Andrew W Mellon Foundation, and Gil Nicol (executive director of IBNA) received US$100,000 from the Exxon Education Foundation, all for IBNA.

The Ford Foundation gave a further US$200,000 in 1968 up to July 1972. This, with other grants, ensured continuation of the project but with some limitations in proposed research. New fundraising initiatives would have to be considered (ISA 1969).

Part VI – Alec Peterson and the establishment of the IB office

Introduction

Part V drew attention to the little-known ISA primary curriculum document; it also outlined the important financial contributions to the IB project, of UNESCO, the Century Fund and the Ford Foundation, during the 1960s and beyond. Part VI pays special attention to the key role played by Alec Peterson and a conference in Sèvres (near Paris) in 1967 at which the decision to continue with the project was taken. This chapter concludes with the creation of the IB office from the ISES, the establishment and membership of its first council of foundation in 1967, and a brief history of the location of the IB office in Geneva up to the present day.

Alec Peterson

Peterson was born in Edinburgh in 1908. While director of the Department of Educational Studies at Oxford, he became part-time director of ISES in July 1966. The involvement of Peterson and Oxford extended the international prestige of the project beyond the group of visionaries clustered around the International School of Geneva. From the late 1950s, the school in Geneva had been engaged in a project with the Department of Educational Studies, Oxford, whereby selected teachers in training were sent to Geneva for a term of teaching practice in an international school (Cole-Baker 1989). Alec Peterson was director of the Department of Educational Studies, Oxford, from 1958 to 1973, where, in the early 1960s, the two main research interests were the structure of the sixth form curriculum and a comparative study of upper secondary curricula and examinations in conjunction with the Council of Europe by Dr W Halls, a member of Peterson's staff. Hence the teacher training and research projects brought first Halls then Peterson into contact with ISA (and later ISES) in the 1960s. Peterson attended his first ISES council meeting in November 1965[1] in Geneva. In connection with his research, Halls had already visited Geneva and had had contact with ISES prior to Peterson's involvement.

Having entered the teaching profession in 1932, during the Second World War Peterson was deputy-director of psychological warfare for South-East Asia Command, serving on Lord Mountbatten's staff; from 1952-54 he was director general of information services during the Malayan emergency. This military background was to provide him with contacts at the highest levels – contacts that greatly assisted the acceptance of the IB by ministries of education and governments. Lord Mountbatten was very influential in this regard and would provide Peterson with a brusque naval introduction: 'Want to know something about the IB? Ask Alec Peterson, one of my wartime spies – always recognise him by his scruffy beard.' (Peterson 1987, p66).

Peterson was Headmaster of government and independent schools in England, the last of which was Dover College, where he had started an international sixth form, before he took up his post at Oxford in 1958. As longtime chair (until 1977) of the editorial board of the prestigious journal *Comparative Education,* he was a recognised expert in that field and a leading pioneer in international education in Britain and beyond (Blackburn 1988). He met Kurt Hahn at a conference on international education in Belgium in 1957 (Peterson 1987, p1). Through this acquaintance with Hahn's educational philosophy and his military connections he visited Atlantic College at St Donat's (Wales), which Kurt Hahn had helped to establish, for the first time in 1961 (before any students had been enrolled). Rear-Admiral Desmond Hoare had been appointed founding Headmaster and Robert Blackburn was deputy-headmaster. (Robert Blackburn went on to become Chief Staff Officer of the London UWC office under Lord Mountbatten from 1968 to 1977. He joined the London office of the IB as deputy-director general from 1978 until his death in 1990.) During the summer of 1962, Peterson worked with Blackburn to provide a broad academic curriculum to the students who were to enter this first of the United World Colleges in September of the same year (Peterson 1987, p9).

Peterson was a staunch campaigner against what he regarded as the over-specialisation of education in England at pre-university level. In 1960 he published a report *Arts and Science Sides in the Sixth Form* based on research funded by the Gulbenkian Foundation. It is noteworthy how closely the content of the report resembles not only the philosophy but also the structure of the IB Diploma Programme, which had only begun to be elaborated a few years later. The Oxford Department of Educational Studies report extolled the need for a broader education that, at the same time, allowed for a degree of specialisation. It spoke of the need for ethics in science and for humanities specialists to know something about the beauty of mathematics. It promoted critical analysis and learning to learn rather than encylopaedic knowledge and memorisation. It proposed increasing the number of specialised subjects in the English sixth form from two to four, spread over the humanities and the sciences. A fifth block of time was to be added to cover religious and physical education, the creative arts and a new course of about 60 hours, which would enable students to 'make a unity' of their whole learning experience. 'The fifth block should therefore include a course, similar to the best and not the worst of the *classes de philosophie*, on the methodology of the subjects.' (Peterson 1987, p42) It is remarkable that this precursor of the ToK course should arise quite independently of the subject of the same name that was first suggested in Paris by Renaud and Tric (previously discussed in Part IV) later in 1965, before either of them had met Peterson.

Peterson's enthusiasm for the IB project is therefore not surprising. Here was the embodiment of an educational ideal he had been unsuccessfully promoting in the UK for so long. His particular interest in the ToK course was the fulfillment of something he had already foreshadowed in the Gulbenkian-funded report of 1960. Peterson had also shown interest in a range of assessment techniques that would gauge 'the whole endowment and personality of the student' (Peterson 1987, p50) and which complemented his curriculum development ideas. His concept of student evaluation, developed over a number of years, later formed part of a study he did for the Council of Europe in 1970. He did not want good teaching to be distorted by intensive examination preparation. He thought highly of oral examinations with a visiting examiner (a hallmark of IB language A, now A1, examinations for many years), of mixing a small amount of multiple choice testing with essays, of assessing analytical skills and cultural sensitivity rather than factual recall, of qualitative measures of affective development (identified particularly through CAS in the IB Diploma Programme).

Peterson was a person of high leverage in educational and diplomatic circles. Said the *proviseur* of the Lycée of St Germain-en-Laye (Paris), the first French school to offer the IB: 'He was a great man of vision.' (Scherer 1992) 'A visionary with charisma. He had the necessary academic standing to make the IB credible. He was very competent and convincing in public.' (Ritchie 1992) Sutcliffe, who retired in 2001 as Head of the United World College of the Adriatic in Trieste, and was a teacher at Atlantic College (where he later was Headmaster) when it opened in 1962, described Peterson as 'rational, imaginative, with fantastic persistence. He was a good speaker and writer who made an enormous contribution. He wanted to broaden the A levels through the IB' (Sutcliffe 1992). 'Peterson had a great reputation. The Ford Foundation accepted him; he had the contacts and the academic standing.' (Leach 1991) 'He was admired by his students. He was concerned about the *whole* person. He was *un sage*.' (Renaud 1991) 'Peterson was very impressive. He had a major role in developing the philosophical underpinnings of the IB. He was *the* outstanding international education figure.' (Gellar 1991) Hanson (1992) describes Peterson as a 'bright, caring, civilised' person who 'disliked the A levels and was educationally attracted to the IB'. Gathier (1992) said: 'Peterson was the backbone, the mental father of the IB. He was devoted and zealous – a continuing source of inspiration. He knew everybody and had good ideas and international contacts.' Carus (1992) said he had 'incredible energy and enthusiasm, and was a phenomenal chairman'. The IB project became firmly established when Peterson became part-time director of ISES from 1966. When the ISES officially became the IB office in 1968, he continued as director until July 1977.

When Peterson was appointed director of ISES in July 1966 he visited Geneva frequently but worked from his office at Oxford University. From January 1967, while on sabbatical leave from Oxford, he lived in Geneva for a little more than six months, in a villa about 100 metres from the IB offices in Cologny. He then resumed his full-time duties as head of the Department of Educational Studies at Oxford with 'the IB as my major research interest' (Peterson 1987, p91). So Peterson was a peripatetic, but extremely effective, part-time director general of the IB. He was based in the UK while Gérard Renaud looked after the Geneva office as deputy director general. Until his retirement in 1973 from Oxford, Peterson used his office there for IB work.

It is a mark of his devotion to education that, after his retirement from Oxford, he moved to London and became a part-time teacher of ToK at Hammersmith and West London College of Further Education from September 1973 where he was provided, at no cost, with 'a largish cupboard which served IB as the office of the director general' (Peterson 1987, p79). The Head of this state school, Bill Bonney Rust, had done research at Oxford and the director of the Inner London Education Authority, Briault, had very much supported Peterson's (and others') attempts to broaden sixth form education in England; Briault had been pleased to authorise the college to take part in the IB experiment. In 1976 Peterson negotiated an agreement with London University's Institute of Education for office space and he spent his last year, 1976-77, there as director general of the IB.

He maintained a fervent interest in the IB until the end. At the council of foundation meeting in November 1988, the year in which Alec died, Robert Blackburn said:

Alec always looked forward. Until the morning of his death (when I had from him two manuscript letters and the copy of a draft speech) he was interested in the introduction of new subjects and new ideas in the IB... He was ... particularly interested in the current debate on the role of internationalism in the IB. Those of us involved might well refer to his brilliant last chapter on the nature of internationalism in *Schools Across Frontiers* (Blackburn 1988).

It is also worth noting that Peterson maintained until the end his interest in reforming secondary education in England. In the year of his death a paper, 'Three decades of non-reform', appeared in the *Oxford Review of Education* (Peterson 1988).

Peterson shaped the educational philosophy of the IB, based on his own deeply humanist and liberal beliefs. This is discernible particularly in the following features: the choice of courses to stimulate the imagination rather than filling the mind with facts, the obligation to do independent research, the balance of academic work and community service, the development of critical thinking skills and the central role of ToK.

A glance through the volumes of Peterson correspondence in the IB's Geneva archives shows just how prodigious he was. Peterson read and wrote French with ease; during the many times when secretarial assistance was at a minimum, there are to be found dozens and dozens of long, very neat, handwritten letters in English and French seeking funding, putting forward educational ideas to curriculum committees and examiners, discussing administrative and political matters concerning the ISES and IB council of foundation, answering queries from schools, alerting an ambassador or a minister for education to the IB project, detailing long-term plans for the future, questioning the budget figures, following up with individuals met at conferences, providing background notes for council agenda items, and so on. In a 1968 message to Goormaghtigh (chair of the IB council at the time) Peterson remarks as an aside: 'I think I am doing about twenty letters a day.' He provided the energy, the pedagogical vision, the educational stature and the administrative competence that gave credibility to the IB project. His contribution was inestimable and his legacy will long be remembered.

Sèvres conference – 1967
After the second curriculum study conference (in October 1965) at Atlantic College, many subject committee meetings took place regularly until 1974. In February 1967 a major IB conference took place at Sèvres for three days, drawing experts from many countries. This conference was to discuss the achievements thus far of developmental work in curricula and examinations by subject committees. Important decisions about the profile of the IB diploma were made. Examination results were to be graded with a minimum total for gaining the diploma, and subject certificates would be given to failed diploma candidates. UNIS representatives also pressed successfully for subject certificates for those wishing to sit individual disciplines and not the full diploma; they believed this would reduce what they saw as elitism in the IB (Peterson 1972, p16-17).

At the conclusion of this conference it was decided to prepare trial examinations from June 1967 until the beginning of a six year experimental period from 1970 to 1975. A number of universities had agreed to accept the IB provisionally, provided the total number of candidates did not exceed 500; several schools would be invited to participate.

After the conference, one American account saw developments as follows: 'The scheme of studies for the IB endeavoured, as far as possible, to combine the intensive study required by GCE A levels with the range and standards for the French baccalaureate, and the flexibility of the American College Entrance Examination Board Advanced Placement examinations.' (Malinowski & Zorn 1973, p165) Mayer, the Twentieth Century Fund consultant, saw it differently: 'The principles on which the IB work was based were Anglo-American in the highest degree.' (Mayer 1968, p215) Although combined British and American representation was greater, there was a considerable French language presence through education officials and university staff from France, Switzerland and Belgium.

This conference gave the IB a mandate to move forward until 1975 (later extended to 1976). The project was elevated to a more serious level requiring planned administration of all its aspects: central programme design and delivery in schools, assuring the quality of the examination process, marketing of the programme to universities, schools, national ministries of education and examining boards, and an on-going evaluation to inform the planning.

Human and material resources, together with further funding had to be found. Of course, these considerations had never been far from the instigators of the project, but it had now taken on a more formal mantel that required appropriate structures. Moreover the initial reactions from schools and universities had been positive; this was motivating to all who believed in it. Everyone knew that the success of the IB diploma rested firmly and squarely on its acceptance by higher education institutions and governments around the world; that meant that the quality of the syllabi, the examination papers and the examiners, had to be beyond reproach. The ideological and pedagogical aims of the IB diploma, as important as they were, would only come to the fore once academic recognition was gained. So, those people of impressive educational and political stature like Goormaghtigh, Peterson and Mountbatten, who had gravitated towards the fledgling IB project, enlisted others of their ilk to promote the credibility of the IB diploma and the IB office.

This conference also proposed the marking scheme from one (very poor) to seven (excellent) for each subject; this has remained. This scale was chosen to provide a more qualitative, rather than quantitative, feel to the assessment. Precise, arithmetic notation of performance such as percentages, were considered to be somewhat unrealistic and often prevented the use of the extreme ends of the arithmetic scales. It was (and still is), for instance, very unusual for a student to receive more than 16 out of 20 for a subject in the French *baccalauréat*; the most brilliant work might obtain a 17 but not a 20. IB examiners were, however, encouraged to use the whole range of grades and to think in terms of the most brilliant work receiving a seven and the poorest a one. This alleviated the 'fear of perfection' that inhabits some examiners who would not give 20 out of 20 or 100 out of 100, but could accommodate giving a seven out of seven (Renaud 2001b).

From the first diploma examinations in 1970 the maximum number of points possible was 44 (seven points times six subjects plus a possible bonus point for the ToK). A student needed 24 points to pass (or 23 at the discretion of the final awarding committee). ToK contributed to the final diploma score from the 1970 examinations in the following way: a mark of six or seven for this subject added one point to the candidate's total while a score of one or two reduced the total by one point (IB 1969b, p5). After the May 1970 examinations a score of 23 was no longer acceptable for passing the diploma even at the discretion of the awarding committee.

The dawning of CAS and the extended essay were discussed at the conference but with a different nomenclature and not in their current state. The origin and development of CAS and the extended essay will be discussed in the next instalment of this history. The ToK course, as previously discussed in Part IV, was confirmed at this conference.

The International Baccalaureate office and its council – 1967

An appropriate administrative entity to manage the trial examinations and the six year experimental period was needed. At the end of September 1967, the ISES council decided to change its title to the International Baccalaureate Office. This reflected more accurately the purposes of the organisation and avoided the term 'syndicate', which had negative connotations in the USA and France (where *syndicat* means 'trade union'). The IB officially changed status from 'association' to 'foundation', with its headquarters in Geneva, under articles 80 *et seq* of the Swiss Civil Code on the 25th October 1968 (Mowat 1968, p286). The IB was created with a mission to administer the examination as had been agreed at the general IB conference at Sèvres in 1967 (IB 1968, p3). It was affiliated with UNESCO as a non-governmental organisation (NGO) in category C (mutual information) in 1970 and moved to category B (information and consultative relations) in 1975 (IB 1975, p11).

There were six full-time IB administrative staff when it was formed in September 1967:

Director	Alec Peterson
Deputy-Director	Gérard Renaud
Executive Secretary	Ruth Bonner
Examination Services	Elisabeth Adossidès
Conference Services	Juliane Willi
Documentation Services	Lucette Donche

Three of the office's main activities are evident in the above distribution of staff. All aspects of examinations needed to be carefully administered; there had to be regular meetings of teachers and examiners, and presentations of the IB to groups of universities, governments, examining boards and schools in different parts of the world. All of this required detailed organisation well in advance (fax machines and email were not available at the time). Production of regulations, subject programmes and teachers' guides, examination papers, examiners' reports and publicity information was an increasing area of documentation activity.

From 1967 the IB consisted of a council of foundation of 20 members,[2] with Goormaghtigh as president, an executive committee and an examinations board, although the organisation was not officially registered as a foundation until 1968.

This tripartite structure was a continuation from ISES, but the mix of actors was not as homogeneous as in each section of ISES. The first council of foundation comprised seven university staff, six education officials, four Heads of school and three non-education professionals. All university academics were professors or directors of university departments in Sweden, Germany, Uganda, Cameroon, Switzerland and Oxford. All were acknowledged experts in their fields and were attracted by the technical aspects of the IB Diploma Programme, together with the ideology concerning world peace and intercultural understanding.

Amongst the high-ranking education officials were Madame Hatinguais, *Inspectrice Générale,* Recteur Jean Capelle, former director of pedagogy in the French ministry of education and Harlan Hanson who, as director of the AP Program, CEEB, was an education official who commanded much respect from universities in the USA. These education officials were attracted because they believed the IB programme was of a very good standard and provided an international experience.

The four Headmasters were from schools involved in the project; two of them, Cole-Baker and Fischer-Wollpert, had been particularly active in curriculum development committees and marketing the IB for ISES. Cole-Baker's original impetus stemmed from concerns about world peace and tolerance of others, university access and the precarious financial situation at the International School of Geneva.

The standing of the three non-educational professionals is impressive. Goormaghtigh has already been discussed in a previous part of this history. Lord Hankey was former British Ambassador to the OECD and a close acquaintance of Mountbatten (Peterson 1987, p26); he played an important role in promoting the UWCs and hence the IB for political and cultural reasons concerned with the promotion of world peace. Louis Armand was a French engineer, former

73

president of the SNCF (*Société National des Chemins de Fer Français*, the government-owned railway system in France) and member of the prestigious *Académie Française* – only individuals at the height of their profession are elected to this body, which was founded in 1635 to protect the French language.

The examinations board of 17 chief examiners (one for each discipline) had nine university staff, six teachers and two education officials (the latter both being inspectors in the French ministry of education) from Britain, Germany, USA, Switzerland, France and Sweden. Bill Halls of Oxford was president.

The IB executive committee was a sub-set of the IB council. It comprised one non-education professional (Goormaghtigh), two Heads of school and two university staff. It considered meeting agendas, discussing the directions to be taken, formulating propositions for the full council, and so on.

The IB office has moved several times in Geneva. As the replacement for the ISES it was housed at chemin de la Chevillarde (adjacent to the International School of Geneva) until October 1967 when it moved to a charming villa at 37 route de la Capite, Cologny. On the 15th August 1970, a further move to larger premises at 12 chemin Rieu, Florissant, occurred with the IB becoming tenants of Union Carbide. The house in Cologny was 'unhappily no longer able to meet the demands of the extension and rationalisation of our administrative work' (IB 1970a, preface). In 1972 the office moved to 1 rue Albert-Gos, still in Champel, when Union Carbide was obliged to recover the space the IB had been renting (Renaud 2001a). On the 14th December 1974, thanks to an offer from the Canton of Geneva, the office moved to the other side of the Lac Léman into the Palais Wilson, 52 rue des Pâquis, where the International Bureau of Education (UNESCO) and the ISA were already located. The gracious Palais Wilson housed the League of Nations from 1920 and was named after its initiator, Woodrow Wilson. The IB office occupied space in this prestigious building until it moved in December 1983 to 15 Route des Morillons, Grand-Saconnex, in close proximity to WHO and the International Labour Office where it remains today.

The director generals of the IB office are:[3]

Alec Peterson 1968-77 (director of ISES from1966)
Gérard Renaud 1977-83
Roger Peel 1983-98
Derek Blackman 1998-99
George Walker 1999-

The next instalment

Part VII will focus on the international consultation that took place in designing the curriculum between the late 1960s and the early 1970s. It will also identify the beginnings of CAS and the extended essay and trace these through to the present day. These two components, along with the ToK (already treated in Part IV of this series), are the most distinguishing features of the IB Diploma Programme, which has stood the test of time. Numerous governments have now introduced compulsory community service in schools and require students to undertake some form of research for the final end-of-secondary school qualification – for example the *Travail de Maturité* in Switzerland. Some countries have also introduced a subject akin to the IB ToK, which inspired, for example, 'Systems of Knowledge' in Malta.

Notes

1. Peterson (1987, p22) says he first came to Geneva in the autumn of 1964 and that approval of the grant from the Twentieth Century Fund had just been announced. It is clear from his own correspondence with Goormaghtigh (chair of the ISES) and the minutes of ISES gatherings that he attended his first meeting in Geneva on 4 November 1965. Moreover the approval for the funding grant occurred in a letter of 8 December 1964 to Cole-Baker, not before, and payment of the grant itself did not commence until early 1965. It might be, therefore, that Peterson misplaced his first visit to Geneva by one year.

2. The first IB executive committee 1967

Chair	Mr John Goormaghtigh
Vice-chair	Dr Heinz Fischer-Wollpert
Secretary	Mr Alexander D C Peterson
Members	Mr Desmond F P Cole
	Prof. Georges Panchaud

3. As at 2010, these details can be updated as follows:

George Walker	1999-2005
Jeffrey Beard	2006-

Dr Nils Andren	Professor, University of Stockholm
M. Louis Armand	of l'Académie française
Prof. Helmut Becker	Director of the Max Planck Instituts für Erziehung, Berlin
Recteur Jean Capelle	Former Director of Pedagogy, Ministry of Education, France
Mr Desmond F P Cole	Director, United Nations International School, New York
Mr J D Cole-Baker	International Schools Association
Prof. Eugène Egger	Director of the Information Centre for teaching and education, Geneva
M. Mohammed El Fasi	Ministry of Education, Rector of Universities, Morocco
Dr Heinz Fischer-Wollpert	Oberstudiendirektor, Goethe Gymnasium, Frankfurt-am-Main
M. John Goormaghtigh	Director of the European Centre, Carnegie Foundation, Geneva
Lord Hankey, KCMG, KCVO	Formerly Permanent British Representative to the OECD
Dr Harlan P Hanson	Director, Advanced Placement Program, College Entrance Examinations Board, New York
Mme Edmée Hatinguais	Inspectrice générale, former Director of the International Centre for pedagogical studies, Sèvres, France
Mr Senteza Kajubi	Director of the Institute of Education, Makerere University College, Uganda
M. Tanyi Mbuagbaw	Director, Pedagogical Institute, Yaoundé, Cameroon
Prof. Georges Panchaud	Professor of Education, University of Lausanne
Mr Alexander D C Peterson	Director, Department of Educational Studies, University of Oxford
M. Charles Sa'd	Principal, National College of Choueifat, Lebanon
M. Jean Siotis	Professor, Graduate Institute of International Studies, University of Geneva
Mme Maria Zakowa	General Inspector, Ministry of Education, Poland

Dr W D Halls	Chair	Oxford University
Dr E Baumann	Physics	Studiendirektor, Karlsruhe, Germany
Dr H R Christen	Chemistry	Cantonal Gymnasium, Winterthur, Switzerland
Dr R F S Creed	Biology	University of London
Prof. U Dahllöf	Psychology	University of Göteborg, Sweden
Dr E Ferguson	Mathematics	Newton High School, Massachusetts, USA
Prof. P Guichonnet	Geography	University of Geneva
Prof. G Lienhardt	Anthropology	Oxford University
Prof. G Mautschka	Music	Music Academy, Frankfort
M. G Ruffino	Latin	Cantonal Gymnasium, Bienne, Switzerland
M. P Trystram	Philosophy	Lycée d'Annemasse, France
Prof. J Vaizey	Political Economics	Brunel University, London
M. A Van Smevoorde assisted by:	Languages	Inspecteur général, France
Mr H Decker		Goethe Gymanisum, Frankfurt
M. J Grunenwald		Inspecteur, Académie de Lille (France)
Dr W D Halls		Oxford University
Prof. G Westin	History	University of Stockholm

(IB 1968, p10-12)

Part VII – IB diploma curriculum design: late 1960s-early 1970s

Part VI focused on the contribution of Alec Peterson, the crucial decision in 1967 to continue with the IB project, and the official establishment of the IB office (later to become the IB organization) in Geneva. This chapter outlines the international breadth of curriculum design and the emergence of CAS and the extended essay – two of the three integral, common components for all students undertaking the IB Diploma Programme.

IB Diploma Programme design continues

More than 50 subject panel meetings occurred between 1966 and 1974 in places including Geneva, Sèvres, Brussels, St Donat's (Wales), Oxford, New York and Paris (Renaud 1974, p56-57). The Twentieth Century Fund, the Ford Foundation and UNESCO grants provided most of the travel costs for these meetings to occur.

Between August 1967 and July 1968 an ISA report on the IB mentioned the following relevant matters. Panel meetings in individual subjects continued to be held in different centres such as Paris, Oxford and New York to develop and refine curricula. Review meetings to assess the results of the June 1967 trial examinations were held in languages (Paris), history (London) and biology (Geneva). USA participants came to Europe. Dr Halls undertook a UNESCO contract to produce a report on equivalence of pre-university programmes in Argentina, Cameroon, Czechoslovakia, France, Philippines, USSR, UK and USA (Pennsylvania). This research would assist the development of IB curricula and examinations. Teachers' guides were published in language A, language B, philosophy and history. 'Physics will be available by September 1968 and chemistry in January 1969.' (ISA 1968b).

A subsequent ISA document for the next year, August 1968 to July 1969, reported on the following matters. An IB mathematics conference was held in Paris and was attended by leading mathematicians from Denmark, France, Germany, Holland, Sweden, Switzerland, the UK and the USA. An IB history conference was held in Copenhagen and a languages conference in Brussels.

The director of the IB office visited multinational schools in the following places and discussed programmes with teachers: Beirut, Copenhagen, Ibadan (Nigeria), Montevideo (Uruguay), New York, Paris, St Donat's (Wales), Santiago (Chile) and Teheran. A team of language and science examiners visited New York, Beirut and Teheran. A major conference on oral examinations was to be held at Sèvres in September 1969. Fifty examiners from nine countries were appointed and 650 candidates registered for the trial examinations of May/June 1969. The hope of Dr Ralph Tyler (Ford Foundation consultant), that the IB would have a positive effect on national curriculum development, was being realised through the following action:

- IB was asked by UNESCO to do a comparative study of pre-university curricula and examinations in six countries;
- IB was commissioned by CERN to plan a model curriculum for a school;
- a large part of the ToK course was being used in the new school programme in Chile; and
- the Académie de Grenoble recognised the IB language B examinations as substitutes for foreign language examinations in the French baccalaureate for students at the International School of Geneva.

The IB project had kept to the planned timetable; the first official examinations would take place in May/June 1970. The IB was providing a valuable laboratory for international cooperation and research on school curricula and transition from school to university (ISA 1969).

In 1970 the first *General Guide to the International Baccalaureate* was published in English and French by the IB. It contained rules, instructions, university recognition agreements and subject programmes for the examination sessions of 1971, 1972 and 1973. Innovative for its day, the following assessment methods were used: course work, written examinations, oral examinations, and practical assessments. The move away from regurgitated knowledge to a more critical, personal approach is nicely stated in this first guide (IB 1970, p22): 'All forms of assessment attempt to bring out not the candidate's ability to memorise, but the extent to which he has assimilated and made his own the subject in which he is being tested.'

English and French were the languages in which all subjects and examinations were provided. It is noteworthy that from 1969 there was also a provision for a school to request the IB to offer one subject from group 3 (the humanities – the 'Study of Man' as it was then called) in a language other than the two IB languages (IB 1969a, p5). The IB would accede wherever possible ... and it did.

For example, some history and economic courses were examined in Danish, Swedish, German and Spanish (then not an official IB language) but the IB did not provide the syllabi in these languages. This continued spasmodically with a very small number of candidates and formally ceased with the publication of the 1985 general guide where this service was no longer offered. (It is worth noting that, beginning in 2003, some 14 German schools overseas began to offer history, biology and the ToK in German as part of a project funded by the German government to provide a bilingual German/Spanish, German/French or German/English IB diploma. In the same year interest in offering a small number of IB diploma subjects in Arabic came from the Middle East and was being discussed.)

Bilingual diplomas were awarded from 1974 to those candidates who presented at least one of their subjects in groups 3 and 4 (humanities and experimental sciences) in a language other than their language A (IB 1972, p20).

Between August 1971 and August 1972 there were five major syllabus revision meetings in maths, economics, languages, history/geography and sciences attended by 108 examiners and teachers from Belgium, Denmark, France, Germany, Iran, Lebanon, Nigeria, Sweden, Switzerland, UK, Uruguay and the USA. As a result the revised *General Guide to the IB* was published in September 1972 (IB 1972a, p5).

This involvement in different parts of the world provided a rich input into the discussions concerning syllabi and examinations. Participants were 'leaders of syllabus reform in their own country who have welcomed both the opportunity to meet with like-minded colleagues and the freedom to establish programmes unhampered by the necessity to compromise with the conservative traditions in national systems' (Peterson 1972, p14).

During the many curriculum and examination development workshops the cultural and educational impact of three major countries was evident: the British brought the essay-type questions; multiple-choice and short answers came from the USA; and in-depth textual analysis and oral examinations were recognised as the French contribution (Fox 1985, p60). But the IB Diploma Programme was not based on the most frequently occurring common aspects of pre-university courses of these and other nations. Those developing courses and examinations were at the forefront of reform within their national systems; the opportunity to exchange creative ideas across national frontiers was an important influential factor for these educational iconoclasts who were dissatisfied with the *status quo* in their own countries. The IB represented an attractive international pilot scheme of innovation in curriculum development and assessment techniques. 'The result has been a series of most stimulating planning meetings and an enthusiastic welcome from the schools concerned.' (Peterson 1971, p5).

Creativity Action Service (CAS)

The precursor of the current CAS was in place by 1968 but it began in the form of a compulsory course 'of theoretical and practical initiation into the Fine Arts' only (IB 1969b, p2) for the equivalent of one afternoon per week. In 1970 the dimensions of 'physical and social service activities' were added. A comment on

80

performance in all three was then required in the annex to the diploma. This first description placed emphasis on active involvement in the aesthetic (doing something creative), the physical (sport, exercise, *etc*) and the social (service within and without the school), and how this was an important contribution to the whole person rather than just a recognition of academic achievement (IB 1970, p14).

The inclusion of social service was largely propelled by Atlantic College where this aspect had been a key element from the beginning, due in no small way to the influence of its founder, Kurt Hahn, and his belief in physical/social activity to develop character. Remarks on the student's completion of this part of the programme and the independent (course) work in most higher level subjects, were made by each school and formed an annexe to the diploma from 1970. The ToK mark awarded by the school was also included as an annexe.

There are inconsistencies in the subsequent general guides. In 1972 there is mention only of creative and aesthetic experience, and the following examples are given: drawing, painting, sculpture, music, dance, drama, film making, dress (IB 1972, p16). Yet students had embarked in some schools on physical and social service activities. In the 1977 *General Guide to the International Baccalaureate* (p18) we find that students should engage in creative, aesthetic or social service activity for the equivalent of one half-day per week. In the 1980 *General Guide to the International Baccalaureate* (p12) the physical and social service components reappear. The acronym CASS (creative and aesthetic activity, and social service – 'physical activity' is mentioned in the text but is not part of the acronym) first appeared in the 1985 *General Guide* (p3 of the 'General Regulations').

In February 1981 Peterson gave a presentation about CASS to a Heads of IB schools' world conference in New York. He stressed active participation, service to others and learning through reflecting on experience. A note from an IB staff member attached to the report of this presentation reads: 'may be distributed to new schools requesting information on CASS' (HSC 1981). This suggests that no formal IB description had yet been developed. As part of the on-going curriculum committees that met for each subject, Robert Blackburn chaired a CASS committee during the 1980s.

In February 1984 Dr Alec Dickson was invited to address a Heads' conference in Geneva on community service. He was the founder of the British-based Voluntary Service Overseas (VSO) and Community Service Volunteers (CSV). He discussed community service with Alec Peterson and Robert Blackburn in London prior to the conference. After his speech he received a number of letters from IB school Heads in which the following message was conveyed: that IB students 'are young people who are enjoying a privileged education with very little awareness of the social and human responsibilities which privilege should entail' (Dickson 1984). The Heads sought more practical guidance on the implementation of meaningful service programmes. Towards the end of 1984 Sir Alec Dickson became an honorary consultant to the IB on CASS activities and visited schools, at their invitation and expense, to give advice (Peel 1984). He died in 1994 at 80 years of age.

CASS became CAS with the publication of *CAS Activities: Guidelines for IBO Schools* (1989). The three parts of CAS were given equal weight whereas previously physical activities had not appeared in the title. 'Action' meant physical exertion in sport, expeditions, mountain climbing, gymnastics, and so on. While community service was encouraged it was realised that in some cultures and geographical locations this was not always easy to accomplish, so the single word 'service' was used to also include service to the school itself; for example, assisting with younger children, organising clubs, environmental awareness action, and so on. 'Creativity' retained the connotations it had had from the very beginning. This was the first curriculum document to explain CAS in some detail to schools.

At the IB Asia-Pacific regional conference in Seoul in 1989, working groups were established to further refine the aims and requirements of CAS. It was decided that the responsibility for the on-going development of CAS should reside in the regions, and that Regional Directors should henceforth chair the CAS committee with staff and school representatives from each IB region. The first CAS committee under this new structure was established in 1990, chaired by John Goodban, regional director for IB Asia-Pacific. This committee produced the first *CAS Guide* in 1991, set up the first evaluation of student performance, and introduced the CAS programme summary questionnaire for schools to complete as part of a new, regular monitoring of CAS by regional offices.

The committee also recommended that CAS requirements must be satisfied before a diploma could be issued and this was agreed by the IB executive committee; the requirements were that students complete a minimum of one half day per week (which some years later was expressed as 150 hours) at CAS over the two years of the IB Diploma Programme and that the school be satisfied with the student's attitude and assiduity. These aspects were in place by 1992. While no 'marks' were gained for CAS, if not satisfactorily completed it disqualified the student from obtaining the IB diploma.

CASS had previously appeared as a compulsory part of the IB Diploma Programme but there was no structure in place to effectively monitor the quality of the CASS experience, which varied considerably, nor to identify unsatisfactory completion of the CASS requirement. From 1992 CAS was established on a more formal and professional basis. The CAS committee produced a new guide in 1996, which was again revised and published in 2001. Both these guides recommended that schools include longer-term community service projects that also incorporated one or both of the other aspects of CAS. For example, I witnessed an activity in Moshi, Tanzania, where IB students dug foundations and made cement blocks for the construction of an education centre and shelter for street children. This combined action with service.

This component of the diploma programme encourages students to participate in sports, artistic pursuits and community service on a weekly basis. In this way young people share their energies and talents while developing awareness, concern and the capacity to work cooperatively with others. 'The IB goal of educating the whole person and fostering a more compassionate citizenry comes alive in an immediate way when students reach beyond themselves and their books' (IB 2001, p3). CAS addresses consideration of the human condition. It is experiential learning followed by reflection. Many CAS projects in schools around the world also promote intercultural understanding and attention to global issues. Students work with refugee families to reinforce the language of the host country and to provide moral support; IB schools in the developing world (or visiting from abroad) assist local schools and villages with books, materials, taking lessons, and inviting local students and teachers into the IB school to integrate with the students who may be expatriates.

In a number of schools IB students provide weekly survival (literacy and numeracy) and recreational programmes for street children in both developed and developing countries. Students in an IB school in Uganda, in collaboration with UNICEF, address the global issue of AIDS through local action. They give weekly moral support to families with HIV positive parents, building up memory banks of the family history and values told by the parents and recorded on tape by the students; this will then be available to the children after the parents have died.

The evaluation of CAS has developed over the years. Currently students are assessed on five performance criteria:

- personal achievement – meeting challenges, participating regularly;
- personal skills – creativity, planning, resource management;
- personal qualities – perseverance, responsibility, self-confidence;
- interpersonal qualities – adaptability, collaboration, empathy, sense of justice; and
- awareness of global issues – ethical appreciation of humanitarian and environmental issues.

(IB 2001, p29)

A CAS review group is now convened, as for all other IB diploma subjects, to revise the guide. The composition of this group includes one staff member from each regional office, one school representative from each region and a representative from the curriculum office in Cardiff.

Extended essay

The extended essay started as 'independent work' that was compulsory in language A and then spread to some other higher level subjects. This was discussed at the 1967 Sèvres conference where it was agreed that it should be marked by the teacher, should form part of the student's school record and be noted on the final certificate (IB 1967).

The first document to use the term 'extended essay' was the *General Guide to the International Baccalaureate* 1970 (IB 1970, p21) where we read in a section on course work that candidates should submit evidence of independent work in higher level subjects such as an 'extended essay' or field work that is assessed by the teacher 'and may be moderated by IBO examiners and will be the basis of the oral examination'. The value of this exercise in developing research skills was the main motivating force and it was also seen as a practical application of critical thinking skills from the ToK course. It provided in addition a degree of specialisation in a diploma profile of breadth and balance.

In the 1972 *General Guide to the International Baccalaureate* (IB 1972, p17), as a result of the problem of student overload, it is stated that a candidate taking three higher level subjects 'each of which involves extended essay work may, with the agreement of the examiner concerned, be permitted to forego the extended essay in one of the three subjects'.

At the 1974 Sèvres conference it was decided to reduce this further: students were required to submit 'one extended essay or project work' in one of the six subjects which would be marked by the teacher, re-marked by an external examiner, and, 'if necessary, the work would be tested further by the cassette oral method' whereby the examiner sent a list of questions to the student who was required to respond orally on cassette and send it back to the examiner (IB 1974, p13). A distinction was now made between course work, which was required in some subjects, and the one extended essay required of each student.

It was not until the 1978 examinations that points were awarded for the extended essay. A mark of six or seven would result in two more points added to the total, while a mark of five would gain the student one more point. A mark of one or two would result in the loss of one point from the total diploma points. In May 1994 the results in the extended essay and ToK were combined for the first time to provide for a mark from zero to three. Schools regarded this as educationally and psychologically more sound since students did not lose diploma points under this revised system, which remains in place today.

The first IB document to assist schools with the nature of this component was *The Complete Guide to Extended Essays*, published in 1992. Prior to that some subject guides gave assistance for extended essays in their area.

The compulsory extended essay of some 4000 words provides students with the opportunity to explore a topic of special interest in one of the subjects being studied for the diploma. It develops independent research and writing skills so necessary for success at university. A teacher supervises the research and the paper is externally examined. Examples of topics (the subject in which the essay was written is indicated in parentheses) are:

- The effects of acid rain on the environment, with a focus on plant life (biology);
- An examination of existing solutions to Latin America's debt crisis in relation to Mexico (economics);
- The contribution of international organisations to the economic development of Geneva (economics);
- Why are the Australian and Singapore stock exchanges more volatile than the major international stock markets? (economics);
- Springtime is silent: the poetry of the Vietnam war (English A1);
- Lillie A James: opportunity and equal rights through education (history);
- The mathematics of nature: the relationship between fractals, chaos and iteration (maths);
- Euthanasia: the morality of killing and letting die (philosophy);
- A study of feminist issues on the Arab Woman (social anthropology);
- Is albinism more prevalent in the African and African American racial groups than in Caucasian and Asian individuals? (biology).

Part VIII – IB trial examinations and experimental period: 1967-76

Introduction

Part VII of this series traced the flurry of curriculum development activities towards the end of the 1960s through to the early 1970s. Of particular importance is the international nature of this curriculum design: many meetings were held in different parts of the world with participants of many different cultures – and it was all organised by the ISES, which then became the IB office in 1967 (officially registered in 1968).

The emergence of CAS and the extended essay, as part of this process, were recounted in some detail, including current information about their compulsory nature and the way they now count towards the total number of diploma points. The importance of CAS in the education of the whole person, a concept dear to Kurt Hahn and Atlantic College, was underscored.

This instalment takes the reader further ahead in time to the trial examinations, then the experimental period, beginning with the first official examinations in 1970 (when some trial examinations were also still being held for some schools). During the experimental period the IB office was functioning principally on external funding from the Twentieth Century Fund and the Ford Foundation with some income in examination fees from participating schools, but no annual subscription fees.

The reader is finally introduced to the first of the syllabuses devised by schools and approved by the IB; this is an excellent example of partnership with schools wishing to offer something specific that complies with the academic rigour, pedagogical practices and educational philosophy of the IB Diploma Programme. School-based syllabuses continue to be offered today and represent quite a variety of disciplines.

Trial examinations 1967-69

In June 1963, four students from the International School of Geneva sat the ISA contemporary history examination. One of these students had been accepted as a sophomore at Harvard (ISES 1964a). Other subjects began to be developed but papers were not set in any subject other than contemporary history until 1967 (Maclehose 1971, p3).

In June 1967 a total of 147 students took trial examinations in history and geography at the International School of Geneva, Latin and physics at Atlantic College and modern languages at both. In May 1968 trial examinations took place as shown below.

Schools and Candidates Participating in Trial IB Examinations 1968

School	No. of Candidates
Atlantic College	169
International School of Geneva	94
UNIS, New York	12
International College, Beirut	48
Copenhagen International High School	8
Iranzamin International School, Teheran	7
North Manchester High School for Girls	11

(Peterson 1972, pp18-19)

These seven schools offered an expanded group of subjects: languages A (literature course for native speakers in English, German, Spanish, Danish or Norwegian) and B (a foreign language course in English, French, German or Spanish), biology, chemistry, economics, history, Latin, mathematics, philosophy and physics.

Trial examinations occurred in 1969 when 720 candidates registered for one or more of the following subjects:

modern languages A & B	physics
history	mathematics
geography	plastic arts
philosophy	music
economics	Latin
biology	classical Greek
chemistry	

The Lycée International de St Germain-en-Laye (Paris) entered 148 candidates with the full approval of the French ministry of education; it had been prevented from taking part in the trial examinations the year before because of the historic events of May 1968 in France. There was a very satisfactory correlation between the results of these students in the French baccalaureate and the IB subjects.

The majority of candidates took certificate subjects only but 18 out of 30 were successful with the full diploma of six subjects (ISA 1969). There were 13 schools taking part. The additional six schools were:

Frankfurt International School
Lycée International de St Germain-en-Laye, Paris

Goethe Gymnasium, Frankfurt
International School, Ibadan, Nigeria
The British Schools, Montevideo, Uruguay
Santiago College, Chile
(Peterson 1972, pp27-28)

Overall 61% of the students passed. A number of candidates had not had an education directly oriented towards the IB, because their schools were still tied to national exams. This was evident in less traditional assessment techniques such as multiple-choice questions where some candidates penalised themselves by guessing. Instead of 'discussing', a number of candidates reproduced facts and statistics or all they knew in any order without an apparent logic to the presentation. Both teachers and students agreed that they preferred examinations that demanded a personal effort of analysis and synthesis rather than simple recall of facts (IB 1969a, p9).

It is interesting to speculate how the various schools became involved. Each will have its own story. Networks between internationally-minded schools spread from the first meeting of the group of that name in 1949 at UNESCO (Paris), its international conference the following year in Geneva, the work of the ISA (for example, Bob Leach visited numerous schools in Asia, Africa and Europe in 1961-62) and its member schools, and its major conference for teachers of social studies in 1962. The newly-formed IB office also engaged in its own marketing (discussed later).

Here is one example of another link. The British Schools, Montevideo, was the first IB school in Latin America and in the southern hemisphere. It was thanks to a chance connection. The Head of the school, Peter Stoyle, did his diploma in education under Alec Peterson at the Department of Educational Studies, Oxford, in the late 1950s. Through this connection Peterson visited the school in 1967 to present the fledgling IB project and there was a positive response. Peter Stoyle retired in 2000 after some 20 years as IB regional director for Latin America.

Experimental period 1970-76

The experimental period of six (later extended to seven) years began in 1970. The conditions of this period were that not more than 500 students per year would do the full IB diploma examination and it would be offered only to a selected group of international schools of high standing officially accepted by the IB. In return, universities offered provisional recognition of the IB diploma. The experiment was to be evaluated by the IB Oxford Research Unit.

Students could present themselves for the full diploma or any number up to five single certificate subjects. (A student taking six subjects, one from each grouping and completing the ToK and CAS, would qualify as a full diploma candidate). Twenty-nine candidates sat for the full diploma and 312 registered for one to five subjects; that is, as certificate candidates in the first experimental examination in 1970 (IB 1975, p23).

The May 1970 examination session was also the last of the trial examinations where, from 1967, any student from a school willing to teach an IB course had been welcome to sit any number of subjects up to six (the full diploma). There were 312 official (29 for the full diploma) and 413 trial candidates; henceforth only students from officially recognised schools could present themselves. So both candidates from officially-recognised IB schools and others presented themselves in 1970. Eleven schools presented candidates for the first official examinations:

United World College of the Atlantic (formerly Atlantic College)
Ecole Nouvelle de Chailly, Switzerland
Copenhagen International School
International School of Geneva
Frankfurt International School
Grännaskolan, Sweden
Iranzamin International School, Iran
The British Schools, Montevideo
Lycée International de Saint Germain-en-Laye, Paris
Lycée Pilote de Sèvres, Paris
United Nations International School (UNIS), New York

Most of this first cohort of 29 diploma candidates (of which 70% passed) were from UNIS; there were no diplomas from the International School of Geneva in that year. Successful diploma graduates gained places at the following universities:

USA – MIT, Parsons, Princeton, Yale
Canada – Toronto
England – London (Westfield College), Oxford (Somerville College), Sussex
(IB 1970b, p20)

From May 1971 only official examinations took place. The following 12 schools entered candidates in May 1971:

School	No. of candidates
Atlantic College, Wales	185
International College, Beirut	23
National College of Choueifat (Lebanon)	1
Copenhagen International School	25
Frankfurt International School	21
International School of Geneva	36
International School of Ibadan (Nigeria)	39
United Nations International School (New York)	60
Iranzamin International School (Iran)	55
Lycée International de Saint-Germain-en-Laye, Paris*	75
Lycée Pilote de Sèvres, Paris*	36
The British Schools, Montevideo (Uruguay)	45
Total	601

*state schools
(IB 1971b, p16)

Lord Mountbatten went to Geneva in September 1971 to present the first IB diplomas to students at the International School of Geneva. During his speech he referred to the fact that Atlantic College had just switched over to the IB Diploma Programme exclusively, because studies in the United World Colleges (of which Atlantic College was the first) were intended to provide an educational programme that would allow young men and women to study together, irrespective of their origins and irrespective of which country they would return to for higher education. He went on to say:

This programme must be really international. It must not reflect the national bias of different nations. No such programmes and examinations existed until the International Baccalaureate was created. This is their great achievement. (IB 1971b, p7)

Schools were, of course, starting the diploma programme two years before presenting candidates. In 1972 the following schools joined those above to register examination candidates:

Ecole Nouvelle de Chailly, Lausanne
Soborg Gymnasium, Denmark*
Goethe Gymnasium, Frankfurt*
National College of Choueifat, Lebanon

Aiglon College, Switzerland
Southampton College, UK*
(*state schools)

Grännaskolan did not continue its involvement beyond the 1970 examinations but renewed its interest more than 20 years later: it has been offering the IB Diploma Programme since 1994. Other schools that feature above for the 1970, 1971 and 1972 examinations are still offering the IB diploma today, except for the following:

- Iranzamin International School disbanded in 1980 after the cultural revolution in Iran;
- Lycée International de Saint Germain-en-Laye ceased to offer the full diploma in 1983 and continued with three or four certificate subjects until 1999;
- Lycée Pilote de Sèvres withdrew in 1985;
- International College, Beirut, withdrew in 1978;
- National College of Choueifat withdrew in 1984;
- International School of Ibadan withdrew in 1992;
- Soborg Gymnasium, Denmark, withdrew in 1975;
- Aiglon College, Switzerland, offered French B until 1997;
- Southampton College, UK, withdrew in 1977;

(Some schools changed names slightly over time; these changes are not recorded here.)

Table 2 below provides statistical information for the experimental period showing the number of candidates, success rates and the number of schools presenting candidates each year.

	1970*	1971	1972	1973	1974	1975	1976	Totals
Number of schools	11	12	19	21	23	30	37	-
Candidates entered	312	601	631	840	1020	1217	1600	6221
Diploma candidates	29	76	151	311	386	377	567	1897
diplomas awarded	20	54	96	236	312	282	433	1433
Certificate candidates	283	525	480	529	634	840	1033	4324
% passes (dip & cert)	69	72	75	76	80	75	75	-
Nationalities	49	50	57	65	71	74	81	-

Table 2: IB Examination Statistics for the Experimental Period 1970-76

* official candidates only
(IB 1975, p23; IB 1976, pp22-23)

The number of different nationalities taking the IB from 1970 to 1976 totalled 104. More than 40 students were represented in each of the following national groups during that time:

USA	271	Fed Rep of Germany	72
UK	222	Uruguay	53
Iran	126	Nigeria	50
Canada	108	Spain	46
France	81	Denmark	41

(IB 1976, p16)

The increase in numbers over this seven-year period is indicative of the interest and satisfaction with the IB diploma courses and examinations. The table does not show the percentage of diploma candidates compared with all candidates who sat, but from 6% in 1970 this rose to a peak of 37% in 1974 and 1975, and was 35% in 1976. This is partly due to the fact that some schools abandoned national curricula and taught the IB exclusively, which was a confirmation of faith in the new international programme.

Five schools were reported to be phasing out nearly all teaching for national exams in favour of teaching the IB exclusively by 1973: Ecole Nouvelle de Chailly (Lausanne), International School of Geneva, Iranzamin International School (Teheran), UNIS (New York) and the UWC of the Atlantic (IB 1970a, p11). The limit of 500 full diploma candidates was not attained during the first six years but was surpassed in the additional year of the experimental period. In 1976 schools entering over 100 candidates (for certificates or diplomas) were:

UWC of the Atlantic, Wales	315
UWC of the Pacific, Vancouver	187
International School of Geneva	143
Iranzamin School, Teheran	141
United Nations International School, New York	124

(IB 1976, p22)

In 1970 the following nine languages were examined as language A: Danish, English, French, German, Hungarian, Norwegian, Persian, Spanish and Swedish. The same group plus Italian and Urdu were examined for language B (11 languages). By 1976, 23 language As were examined and 28 language Bs including Arabic, Czech, Dutch, Finnish, Hebrew, Hindi, Indonesian, Japanese, Malay, Polish, Portuguese, Russian, Serbo-Croat, Thai and Turkish. This is indicative of the geographical spread of the IB and of the multicultural nature of the student population in the international schools.

The average pass rate over the seven years was 75%, which is not unduly high when one considers that almost 500 candidates in 1976 came from the two UWCs where students around the world are selected for scholarships largely on academic merit.

Table 2 shows a healthy growth situation with 1433 IB diplomas awarded by 1976. The vast majority of these (approximately 97%) gained immediate admission to universities. What is more important is that there was a growing number of students (6221) who had direct experience of the IB and would spread the word to others. Similarly, teachers and Headmasters in 37 schools around the globe (by 1976) were contributing to international diffusion of the programme.

By the end of 1972 the experimental period was already exhibiting signs of success.

> From the first it was intended that the project should provide an opportunity as well as a challenge to the spirit of international cooperation by bringing together teachers from schools and universities in many countries in the practical context of a common endeavour to meet a common educational need. These hopes have to a considerable extent been realised in the first three years. (IB 1972a, p5).

The experiment had to remain manageable by limiting the number of schools and candidates admitted (no more than 500 diploma students), their geographical distribution, the areas of research, and the extent of university recognition. 'The experiment seems to show that the instrument has functioned correctly but it needs the support of inter-governmental collaboration to develop its potential.' (IB 1973, p6). A word of caution was sounded about maintaining intellectual autonomy, if the IB were controlled by governments, to guarantee the pursuit of pedagogical objectives and not of political advantage.

From 1970 to 1974 the total possible maximum points for the diploma was 43 (including one point for a high score in the ToK) and students needed 24 points to pass. From 1975 until 1977 this possible total rose to 50 points (including one mark for a high score in the ToK) to accommodate students who presented seven subjects; they needed 28 points to pass. From 1978 until 1986 the maximum points for a student presenting seven subjects rose to 52 with the addition of a maximum of two bonus points for the extended essay. From 1987 seven subject diplomas were no longer awarded (IB 1987, p40); a seventh subject could be taken as a certificate in addition to the diploma of six subjects plus the ToK, the extended essay and CASS.

So from 1987 the 45 point diploma was established and students required 24 points to pass, or more if there were very low scores in a number of subjects. This remains so today. In 1992 the IB introduced a new system where diploma points would no longer be deducted: depending on the combined total of the ToK and the extended essay marks, a student could be awarded zero, one, two or three diploma points. This was first applied in the May 1994 examination session.

School-based curriculum development

By 1968, in the sixth subject area of the IB, students could choose one of the following: an arts subject, a third language (classical or modern), a second subject from the 'Study of Man', or the experimental sciences, or a syllabus submitted by the school and approved by the IB (IB 1968, p5). This provided for curriculum development at school level, and this has remained an important element of the IB Diploma Programme. As at November 1973, 11 school-based subjects had been developed and accepted:

- Arts – drama, film-making, contemporary music;
- Study of Man – Middle-East societies, comparative regional studies, political theory, the UN and disarmament/aggression;
- Interdisciplinary – environmental studies, marine studies, photographic science, astronomy

(IB 1973, pp41-45)

These were internally assessed but externally moderated by an IB examiner. Complete syllabus statements were produced and printed by the IB for other interested schools. Some of these were later to become adopted and developed by the IB as fully-fledged diploma subjects: for example music in 1979, environmental systems in 1989, and theatre arts in 1996. Film took much longer to emerge and was developed on a trial basis by the IB as an integral part of the IB Diploma Programme for the first time in 2001.

During the February 1978 second inter-governmental conference in London, a report was given on school-based curriculum development. Applied chemistry was being developed at the International School of Geneva and nutritional science in Singapore (Peterson 1978, p164). Maths studies (for non-mathematicians) was being pioneered at Atlantic College with a grant from BP (IB 1978a, p2).

Currently the following school-based syllabuses have been approved and are examined each year:

accounting	Fijian studies
agricultural science	historical and contemporary
ancient Greek civilisation	Brazilian studies
ancient history	nutritional science

art history

Asian arts

beginners' Nynorsk

Brazilian studies

Chile and Pacific basin

Chinese studies

Classical Greek and Roman studies

electronic music

electronics

European studies

peace and conflict studies

political thought

science, technology and society

social studies

Turkish social studies

United States history

world cultures

world politics and
international relations

world religions

All school-based syllabuses are at standard level (SL – formerly subsidiary level) and are taken by a very small percentage of all examination candidates. There are strict conditions in presenting a syllabus to the appropriate IB committee for acceptance: it must have a certain academic rigour, concur with IB objectives, and be examinable on a par with other established SL subjects.

Some school-based syllabuses are very much in tune with the pedagogical objectives of the IB Diploma Programme: they are more related to the application of knowledge, more culturally based, more interdisciplinary and more international than some of the fully-fledged IB subjects. The problem is their credibility *vis-à-vis* university recognition. Since many of them do not fall into a recognisable discipline of academic standing, they are not readily accepted by all universities. This is a major contributing factor to the small number of students who enrol in these subjects.

At the end of his book, Peterson (1987, p202) asked whether the total IB diploma curriculum 'could not be better adjusted to the needs of the whole person without sacrificing either the role of the rigorous academic disciplines... or the acceptability of the IB diploma for entry to universities...'. He suggested that the answer might lie in a different type of SL subject that was not simply a less academically demanding version of its higher level (HL) counterpart of the same name. His proposal was that there should be SL subjects that are not necessarily preparatory to further study but which conclude with the diploma examinations, and he took the variety of school-based syllabuses as an illustration of what he meant. The IB has been moving in this direction by piloting three interdisciplinary subjects at standard level from 2001:

- Text and performance (groups 1 and 6: literature and the arts);
- Ecosystems and societies SL (groups 3 and 4: humanities and experimental sciences);
- World cultures SL (groups 3 and 6: humanities and the arts).

It is worth remembering that three interdisciplinary school-based syllabuses already existed by 1973, as noted above. In this way, the school-based syllabuses also serve as a stimulus for formal IB creative curriculum initiatives.

Part IX – Evaluation of the IB project 1967-76

Introduction

In the early years a number of feedback mechanisms were put in place to monitor progress and inform decisions about the future viability of the IB Diploma Programme project. Of great importance were the design of the curricula and their delivery in schools, examination processes and their reliability and validity, university recognition, and the IB's administrative procedures. This chapter relates to the evaluation of the experimental period from 1967 until 1976, which was discussed in the previous chapter.

Oxford Research Unit

The IB Oxford Research Unit was the formal apparatus to conduct evaluative research; at times national education authorities took an interest in matters such as the statistical analysis of correlations between the IB and final degree results in UK universities, which was carried out by the London-based Schools Council in 1979 (Renaud 1974, p20). The Oxford Research Unit analysed IB examination results, compared them with national examination results, followed up students at university, contributed to the development of curricula and assessment techniques, and undertook special IB research projects as required. The researchers were IB employees.

Through Peterson and Bill Halls, the Oxford Department of Educational Studies became a research centre for the IB project, working together with the ISES (and later the IB office). Prior interest had already been expressed by Bill Halls who had attended the March 1964 Sèvres conference of the European Teachers Association, French Section, representing the Oxford Department of Educational Studies. Oxford had been there because of their research into sixth form curriculum in Britain and a comparative study of pre-university courses across Europe; the Institut Pédagogique de Sèvres was interested in a broader-than-European baccalaureate. Halls had also attended the ISES special council meeting in Geneva on 13 November.

The Oxford Research Unit was established within the Department of Educational Studies at Oxford in 1967. Dr Bill Halls, who had been working on an Oxford/Council of Europe study of curricula and examinations, was appointed director and remained so until 1972. The unit had a house at Oxford at its disposal, rent free. As at May 1971 it had completed the following work: statistical analysis of IB examination results, comparisons of IB results with national examinations (for students who sat both), follow-up of students at university, the development of interdisciplinary courses, and the establishment of trial taxonomies of objectives for history and biology (IB 1971a, p7).

The IB Research Unit at Oxford continued with a number of activities during the 1972-1973 school year. The annual statistical analysis of IB examination results included reports on the distribution of marks, mean scores, variance, and the correlation between written and oral examinations and school assessment. The follow-up study of IB diploma holders was being done by Mr Stephens, IB universities liaison officer, using three questionnaires. In the first the student provided information concerning his or her personal record – previous schools, languages spoken, future plans for education – and an opinion on the value of his or her IB studies. The second questionnaire was completed by the student's IB school to provide information concerning the student's general background and health, choice of IB subjects, attitude and intellectual standard. The third questionnaire was completed by the student at the end of the first year at university; it sought comments on progress and the advantages and disadvantages of the IB programme as compared to the national programmes of fellow students. A test of ethnocentricity was given to diploma candidates. Information on the creative, aesthetic and social activities of diploma candidates compared with those who had followed national programmes was also pursued.

For 1972-1973 the Research Unit was reorganised under the direction of Dr Kevin Marjoribanks, replacing Halls who had to devote time to the increasing amount of research in other fields. A steering committee was set up under the chairmanship of Alec Peterson. Other members of staff included Mr L Stephens, universities liaison officer and Mrs A Hampton, curriculum development officer who worked in Geneva (IB 1973, pp12-13). The Research Unit consisted of paid personnel who were almost all university academics like Halls and Majoribanks. Halls had already undertaken research for the Council of Europe on university entrance criteria across Europe; the IB project promised to provide at least part of the answer to international mobility and university entrance.

In July 1974 the Oxford Research Unit closed down, although it was to have monitored the IB during the six-year trial period from 1970 to 1975. Majoribanks left to take up the Chair of Education at Adelaide University, Australia, and the responsibility for evaluating the final year of the project was transferred to Geneva (IB 1973a).

Consultative committee

Another formal structure provided feedback after each examination session: the consultative committee. It was regarded as a friendly dialogue between the 'producers' (IB staff and examiners) and the 'consumers' (students and teachers). 'Students' opinions were expressed in a mature fashion, resulting in a number of extremely useful suggestions for improvement' (Renaud 1974, p28). The first meeting took place at CERN, Geneva, on 7 June 1969, and brought together 40 participants: IB staff, teachers, students, and examiners. A sample of some comments from this first meeting follow (IB 1969a, pp12-13):

'Oral examiners were not all of the same quality, and it would help to have two examiners present, one outside examiner and one teacher from the school. Oral examiners should be given the maximum of information on the candidate, stressing in particular his strong points.' (a student)

'We are pleased to see such a vast improvement in the examinations this year. Generally speaking, the standard of each paper seemed to be satisfactory to us... Subsidiary Level, if anything, was a little easier than we had anticipated (or feared) but we think it is about the right level.' (a teacher)

'This baccalaureate demands more reflection than pure knowledge and generally comprises a good choice of questions.' (a student)

'I expect candidates to support their answers with reasoning; indeed this is one of the reasons for having fewer questions in the paper than was originally proposed.' (a mathematics examiner)

The next meeting occurred again in Geneva on the 26th and 27th June 1970. Matters raised included:

- clarification of directives from teachers to students concerning IB requirements;
- the advantages and disadvantages of oral examining by cassette;
- examination procedures concerning the creation of exam questions, notation;
- the choice of vehicular languages, the possibility of obtaining corrected specimen papers;
- spreading the IB course over three years to alleviate the workload on students;
- problems related to geographical location such as postal delays in receiving examination papers; and
- despatch procedures for returning papers, lack of sophisticated communication networks in some countries.

Each subject and its examination came under scrutiny and comments were conveyed to the chief examiners when the latter were not present at the consultative committee meeting. Sample comments from this session were:

'The IBO should have a (northern hemisphere) autumn examination for those who fail one or two subjects or for those who wish to improve their mark.'

'The history course and examination is too biased towards the West. There is not enough about Asia, Africa and South America.'

'My main impression about the IB is that it is not sufficiently original or innovative at a time when the tendency of universities is to move towards a student evaluation comprising information outside the formal academic results.'

These comments are from the *IBO Semi-Annual Bulletin* of November 1970 (IB 1970b, pp14-15); the derivation of each statement was not indicated as it had been in the issue of the previous year.

The third consultative committee meeting took place on the 26th and 27th June 1971, again at CERN, with 57 participants: 14 students, 28 teachers representing 12 schools, six examiners and nine members of the IB administration (IB 1971b, p17). The next meeting took place in June 1972 at Atlantic College with 62 participants from the IB council and administration, examiners, teachers and students (IB 1972, p5). Subsequent IB bulletins contain no record of any further meetings of the consultative committee, nor does the literature concerning the IB. Renaud and Bonner recall that this method of feedback lasted only 'three or four years' and not for the whole of the experimental period (Bonner 1991; Renaud 1991).

Other feedback

Evaluation was naturally integrated into the process in other ways, particularly via the subject meetings, and it occurred informally as events succeeded each other. 'All in all, the experiment, confined initially to a relatively restricted sphere, developed pragmatically as it was put into practice.' (Renaud 1974, p28). A number of factors contributed to the effective execution of the IB programme: the limited scale of the venture, frequent feedback, the rapid introduction of amendments (as a result of feedback), and the independence from political or administrative pressure, allowing uninterrupted focus on educational objectives.

The Gulbenkian Foundation funded an IB research project to investigate whether the IB programme developed a wider interest and involvement in creative and aesthetic activity. Eight IB schools from Geneva, Lausanne, London, Wales, New York, Teheran, Montevideo and Paris took part in the study. Over a two-year period, spanning the 1974 and 1975 examination sessions, 255 IB diploma holders were interviewed (Hampton 1976, p271). The analysis showed a slight but definite trend of IB diploma holders towards the attributes of conceptual ability, aesthetic appreciation, creative involvement and a liking for independent study.

Other positive and negative feedback emerged. The academic standard of the IB was thought to be challenging. 'The IB is more demanding than the new German university entry qualification,' said Egger (1981, p7), a member of the Swiss Commission of UNESCO. 'The higher level subjects are usually more rigorous than the same subject in the final two years of a national system,' said the director of the French Secondary Section at the International School of Geneva, P Decorvet (1981, p55). Students and teachers saw it as an intellectually challenging programme, which developed critical thinking and whose methods, particularly research papers and oral examinations, were appealing. It could be taken in two languages (three from 1982) and the world literature of languages A gave important cultural insights. The history course emphasised a non-national approach and had a good effect on attitudes concerning international cooperation; it developed a real understanding of other countries' problems. Most importantly it was rapidly being recognised by universities worldwide.

Dissatisfaction was also expressed by teachers and students. The content of subjects was thought to be too vast resulting in superficial investigations of significant topics. There was a lack of emphasis on sports and the arts. The second language requirement was considered unreasonable for students arriving from the USA, for instance, where no second language requirement existed; it took at least three years to acquire the IB language B subsidiary (now 'standard') level if starting without any second language knowledge. Some teachers also criticised the high cost, complicated administrative procedures and communication difficulties with the IB, particularly for geographically distant schools. This feedback assisted the IB to modify the programme and its administration as it thought appropriate and as funds would allow.

Sèvres conference 1974
This conference had been suggested at the 1967 Sèvres meeting in order to take stock of progress during the experimental period. It occurred at the Centre International d'Etudes Pédagogiques, Sèvres, Paris, from 22 to 26 April 1974, and was attended by 64 people from 21 countries. The French ministry of education funded it and UNESCO assisted by providing a list of experts to invite. The aim was to study the conditions and results of the IB experiment to see:

1. whether it should be transformed into a long-term operation; and

2. what were the desirable future developments and procedures.

Three commissions were established to deal with policy and administration, syllabi, and methods of assessment.

The conference took no formal decisions but gave advice and made recommendations. 'It was then up to the IBO to follow up these recommendations by approaching national authorities or inter-governmental bodies.' (Renaud 1974, p31). On the first question the conference recommended that the IB become a permanent operation and make the IB Diploma Programme available in the greatest number of countries, representing the widest diversity of culture and educational tradition, especially in the developing countries (Renaud 1974, pp29-30). On the second question, concerning future directions, the conference made recommendations in four areas: acceptance of schools into the programme, aims of the IB, future support, and geographical expansion.

It was noted that more than 80 international schools were on a waiting list to participate in the IB after the experimental period (IB 1974, p9). Four main types of client schools should be considered:

- schools designated 'international' (that is, catering for a variety of nationalities from internationally-mobile families) whose teaching must take into account the cultural diversity and mobility of students;
- pilot schools chosen as experimental centres within a national system for testing of new programmes and methods;
- experimental sections within national establishments, parallel with traditional sections (as in France and the Netherlands); and
- schools wishing to adopt the IB such as national state or private schools.
  (Renaud 1974, p31).

The IB was seen as being of value in avoiding cultural isolation of immigrants whereby they could participate in a method of teaching and evaluation that had some similarities with their earlier preparation in their country of origin. It was considered particularly relevant in countries with minority problems that are often basically linguistic in character.

A major aim of the IB should be to provide access to higher education around the world; the conference hoped that the few countries denying recognition of the IB for access to university by their own nationals would do so soon. (France lifted this restriction towards the end of the 1970s and Germany did the same in 2000.) The second major aim should be to broaden courses beyond a challenging academic orientation towards some post-secondary vocational

102

training. (Interestingly, it is only since 2004 that the IB began seriously exploring the option of some vocationally-oriented courses at the Diploma Programme level.) The conference recognised that the aims of the IB had evolved and would continue to evolve with the operation. Aims reflect the action to be taken to reduce or avoid what is seen as a 'problem'. Initially the IB was to assist internationally-mobile students to gain university access around the world and to provide a new type of international education, which was lacking for students in multicultural environments. As the courses developed and teachers and other educators from many countries met, the value of the IB for national schools began to appear. It could assist national systems by stimulating research into new curricula, teaching methods and examination techniques. The IB could also provide to those nations who wanted it an education programme that was already operating in schools in a number of countries and would bring an international dimension to national programmes (IB 1974a, p14). Thus national education officials began to realise that there was a problem in national schools: lack of an international experience in the curriculum. This aspect of the IB had been expounded by Peterson at the 1968 ISA annual conference. He spoke of his interest in the IB to assist student mobility and to reform national systems, in particular sixth form education in Britain. The need for an international curriculum perspective had been mooted as far back as 1924 but in conjunction with international schools; the shift was to now offer such a perspective to national schools.

Mr Stephens, university liaison officer with the IB, reported that 92% of the 400 IB diploma holders admitted into more that 200 universities in 25 countries had been followed up. Good academic results, general open-mindedness and adaptability were features of these students (IB 1974a, p13). In terms of educational return on the investment both for students and for influencing national systems, the IB project was deemed successful, but new funding initiatives would need to be found before the end of 1976 when the major grant money would be used up.

Part X – School Heads and governments rescue the IB project

Introduction
After the positive evaluation of the IB trial and experimental period, described in the last chapter, new funding had to be found for the continuation of the project beyond 1976. In addition to the establishment of a trust fund in the UK, UNESCO was asked to underwrite and take responsibility for the whole operation. Neither of these initiatives amounted to anything, but the creation of the Standing Conference of Governments (SCG) and the Heads Standing Conference (HSC) were significant events that enabled the project to continue and flourish.

UK trust fund
Foreseeing the need for future funding, Peterson, Lord Hankey[1] and Blackburn signed a declaration in 1970 for the establishment of an IB fund in the United Kingdom with the following purposes:

- to promote and administer an international examination giving access to higher education around the world;
- to undertake research and disseminate it in relation to the foregoing objective;
- to cooperate with any non-governmental, governmental or intergovernmental institution concerned with curricula development, pedagogy and examination techniques.
  (IB 1970c)

The trust deed speaks of the power to issue appeals for donations. Since 1970 a number of foundations did provide funds but these funds passed via the Geneva office as they were not from benefactors in the United Kingdom. The last statement, issued by the IB auditors in 1995, said that to the best of their knowledge no income had ever been collected in this fund.

The IB as part of UNESCO
The 1974 Sèvres conference had suggested that the IB should be integrated with UNESCO and that decentralisation should occur; this would make available local UNESCO officers to meet the requirements of more numerous schools and colleges in particular geographical areas such as the USA and the UK (Renaud 1974, p31-33). This meant that UNESCO would give a long-term commitment of support, oversee and underwrite the whole IB operation.

In November 1974 Peterson and Renaud attended the 18th general conference of UNESCO asking for the IB to come under UN control from 1977 (Peterson 1972, p31). Fourteen countries proposed that the Director-General UNESCO examine the possibility of contributing to the continuation of the IB office and submit a proposal to the next (19th) general conference. The countries were Canada, Egypt, UK, Iran, Switzerland, Uruguay, Malta, Morocco, Mauritius, Mexico, Nigeria, Tanzania and Togo. The 70 delegations present accepted this with a unanimous vote. The actual resolution recognised the considerable progress in devising a common programme and standards across nations at upper secondary level, and access to universities worldwide. The proposers hoped that this service to many nations could be reinforced under the international control of UNESCO.

This did not occur and a number of reasons have been suggested. For Leach, UNESCO's main work was to compare national education systems and to provide means of improving the education system in individual countries through the exchange of information and people. From its beginning in 1945 one of its principal projects had been to eradicate illiteracy. 'Although an international organisation, UNESCO recognised education as a national prerogative.' (Leach 1969, p6). Peterson agrees with Leach and thought UNESCO rejected incorporating IB into its structure:

... possibly because there is no tradition within UNESCO of actually operating in the field of education as it does in the fields of science and culture, through independent organisations either existing or set up for the purpose. UNESCO seems always to have regarded education as a matter for the member states. (Peterson 2003, p97).

At the second IB inter-governmental conference (see the next section of this chapter) in London in 1978 the Secretary of State for Education and Science, Shirley Williams, said that UNESCO did not have the resources to take on the IB project (IB 1978a). At the third IB inter-governmental conference in 1981 in Brussels, Goormaghtigh said: 'UNESCO, the only relevant inter-governmental organisation, decided the IB was better left to a separate foundation' (IB 1981a, Annex III). UNESCO certainly had other priorities. Moreover the IB would not have developed as independently as it had, were it to be subjected to UNESCO control. UNESCO's political, ideological and cultural context prevented it from engaging in an international education venture, when its main purpose was to assist national education in each country through exchanges of information and ideas. To have taken on the IB would have been to deny, to some extent, the value of the national systems UNESCO set out to improve.

105

It was also realised that, although belonging to UNESCO might provide continuous funding, the educational independence of the IB and the ability to respond nimbly and appropriately to world trends in education would be seriously compromised through the inevitable bureaucratic machine of UNESCO, as it tried to manoeuvre between the competing demands of its member states.

The creation of the Standing Conference of Governments (SCG)
In 1964 Russell Cook, ISA chairman, suggested stimulating national government support for international schools (ISA 1964, pp10-11). This marks the first recorded initiative by ISA to seek national government sponsorship for international schools on the basis that the citizens of particular countries are living abroad and this is therefore a legitimate expense. Cook suggested that it would be necessary to ascertain the number of governments subsidising *national* schools abroad and to what extent such sudsidies might conflict with those to be attributed to international schools. At the time the idea went no further but it was later revived by the IB and, for some years, provided a substantial part of the funding for that organisation.

Piet Gathier, director general of secondary education in the Netherlands, joined the IB council in 1974 at the invitation of Leo Fernig of UNESCO. When it became increasingly unlikely that integration with UNESCO would take place, Goormaghtigh looked at alternative methods of securing inter-governmental support. Piet Gathier persuaded the Netherland's minister of education to call the first Inter-governmental IB conference in the Hague in February 1976. Eleven countries pledged funding for the next two years: Belgium, Canada, Denmark, Italy, Morocco, Netherlands, Switzerland, UK, USA, Finland and Germany. This meant that a third of the IB's budget was provided by a group of UNESCO member states; it marked the beginning of a period of government funding (IB 1975a). An important political development had now occurred: IB moved from being a totally independent foundation in Geneva to an organisation partly supported by UNESCO member states.

In February 1978 the second inter-governmental IB conference was held in London at the invitation of Shirley Williams, Secretary of State for Education and Science. Opened by HRH The Prince of Wales, this conference attracted twice the number of governments as in the Hague two years before. Delegations at ministerial or other high official level attended from Australia, Belgium, Canada, Denmark, Finland, France, Federal Republic of Germany, Greece, Hong Kong, Hungary, Italy, Japan, Kenya, Malaysia, Mexico, Morocco, Netherlands, Nigeria, Norway, Poland, Portugal, Saudi Arabia, Senegal, Spain, Sri Lanka, Tanzania, Sweden, Switzerland, United Kingdom, USA, USSR and Venezuela – 32 countries in all.

At this meeting Goormaghtigh proposed the creation of a Standing Conference of Governments (SCG) whose members would each contribute a sum of US$15,000 per year to the IB. This suggestion was adopted as a resolution. Eight of the members of the SCG would be nominated to the IB council of foundation, thus forming a third of that body, the other two thirds being representatives of the HSC and the executive committee of the IB. Delegates welcomed this resolution 'as setting a new precedent for structuring international cooperation in education without creating a new network of legal obligations or a new bureaucracy' (Peterson 1978, p164). At the conference dinner, speeches were made by Lord Donaldson, Minister for the Arts, by the Minister for Education of Senegal, by the Deputy Secretary-General of the Commonwealth and by Earl (as he then was) Mountbatten of Burma. The creation of the SCG had the blessing of some very influential people and there was now the promise of a much more stable financial base than that provided only by donor organisations.

A significant number of governments saw the IB as an innovation of great service to both international schools and national schools, by providing fresh ideas on curriculum development and examining which could prove to be important for national systems.

The SCG elected nine people to sit on the IB council of foundation and two of these, usually the chair and vice-chair, sat on the executive committee. The following people have been elected chairs of the SCG since its foundation in 1978:

1978-1984: Piet Gathier, director general of education, The Netherlands.

1984-1988: Jean Dumortier, secretary general, Ministry of Education for French-speaking Belgium.

1988-1993: Bengt Thelin, former director general of education, Sweden.

1993-1996: Mrs Zoe Pohjanvirta, government counsellor, Finland.

1996-2000: Raymond Jourdan, Head of the Collège Claparède in Geneva, Swiss representative to the Council of Europe.

2000-2001: Mrs Haifa Dia Al-Attia, education advisor to HRH Princess Sarvath, Amman, Jordan.

By 1987 there had been a decline in the financial support from governments; this led to a new form of collaboration whereby membership of the SCG meant either contributing financially or undertaking activities that would promote IB programmes in the country. The SCG met annually at the same time as the council of foundation and nine of its members were elected to the council for a three year term.

From May 2001 a new Government Advisory Committee (GAC) was formed by the director general and the SCG ceased to function. The GAC consists of ten senior civil servants or advisers on education in diverse government systems appointed by the director general for an intial two year term. The purpose of the group is to further promote IB-government cooperation in a number of ways, which include: official recognition of IB programmes, pedagogical exchanges of ideas, research of mutual interest, setting up pilot projects in state schools in developing countries, teacher training, IB input into national education reforms seeking to internationalise the curriculum.

The creation of the Heads Standing Conference (HSC)
The money from the Ford Foundation grant expired in 1976; after that, the IB had to find alternative funding. The IB council was depending very much on UNESCO to provide financial support for the next two years of operation in conjunction with funding from national governments but, on 14 May 1976, UNESCO's executive board decided not to do so. The future of the IB became critical from that moment. Peterson wrote immediately to all schools associated with the IB, commencing with the following sentence:

> It is with the most profound regret that I am compelled to notify all schools ... that unless an additional $130,000 a year for the years 1977 and 1978 can be assured before July 15 of this year the decision to close down the project will be taken on that date ...
> If [negotiations] should prove unsuccessful, the IB Office will close down on July 31 [1976] for all operations other than the administration of the 1977 examination and the completion of any separately funded development projects. (Peterson 1976a).

As a result of the circular, a meeting of ten Heads,[2] representing the schools that had been with the project the longest, took place on the 4th of June 1976 with Peterson at his London office. At the meeting Peterson suggested schools contribute 2000 Swiss francs per year but Gellar said that it should be 10,000 Swiss francs and this was supported by all those present. This was accepted and an annual school subscription to the IB, in addition to the exam fees, began in 1976 (Gellar 1991). Peterson acknowledges that this meeting was a turning point that assured the future of the project (Peterson 2003, p94). Until that time schools teaching the IB Diploma Programme paid only an examination fee because the project was in an experimental stage (until 1976) financed largely by the Twentieth Century Fund, the Ford Foundation, a number of small UNESCO contracts and grants from various other sources. Lejeune suggested that the Heads of IB schools should meet in 1977 and proposed Geneva as the venue. This was accepted.

In March 1977 the HSC was formed at the Palais des Nations at the initiative of Monsieur René-François Lejeune following the 1976 London meeting with Peterson (IB 1977a, p25). School Heads came together to determine the mode of financial participation together with the government group that had met for the first time in 1976. Pedagogical and administrative exchanges were also facilitated.

During the 1978 London inter-governmental conference Peterson reported on progress during the last two years. Exam entries were at almost 2400 per year and rising. Since 1970 almost 9000 students of 108 nationalities had taken the IB examinations and approximately 6000 students were following the IB curricula (Peterson 1978, p163). This increase in participating schools gave more financial stability to the IB office.

Heads saw the educational potential of the IB in gaining university access and in offering an international programme, which they needed for the internationally-mobile student body in their schools. They wanted the IB to continue and valued its service to such an extent that they were now willing to pay for it.

The HSC comprises all the Heads of IB schools. A Heads Representative Committee (HRC) of nine was elected with power to co-opt a further six members for a three year period, renewable once. The HRC represented the IB schools in the governance of the organization and four of its members sat on the executive committee. The following Heads have been chairs of the HRC since it was founded in 1977:

1977-1978: René-François Lejeune, International School of Geneva

1978-1984: Phil Thomas, International School of Geneva

1984-1986: Jacqueline Roubinet, Ecole Active Bilingue Jeanine Manuel, Paris

1986-1989: Michael Maybury, Vienna International School, Austria

1989-1992: Bob Pearmain, Winston Churchill High School, Alberta, Canada

1992-1996: Leif Berntsen, Copenhagen International School, Denmark

1996-1999: Robert Snee, George Mason High School, Virginia, USA

1999-2001: Margaret Nkrumah, SOS-Hermann Gmeiner International College, Ghana

International Heads Representative Committee (IHRC) from 2001:[3]
2001-2003: Malcolm Lamb, Pembroke School, South Australia
2003-: Tony Flatley, Collège Esther-Blondin, Quebec

The HRC met two or three times a year and nine of its members were elected to the council of foundation; this gave a third of the voting rights. As one of its tasks it organised world conferences of Heads of IB schools; these have been held, at first annually, and since 1994 every two years. Conferences have taken place as follows:

> Geneva 1977 and 1978, Vienna 1979, Geneva 1980, New York 1981, Geneva 1982, Madrid 1983, Geneva 1984, Quito (Ecuador) 1985, Paris 1986, Washington DC 1987, Geneva 1988, Singapore 1989, Anaheim (USA) 1990, Barcelona 1992, Buenos Aires 1993, Ottawa 1994, Jakarta 1996, Montreux 1998, Ghana 2000, Cancún (Mexico) 2003, Bangkok (2005).

A conference was to have been held in Nairobi in 1991 but was cancelled because of the Gulf War. In spite of the cancellation notices two Heads appeared at the appointed time and one of them came from as far away as Australia. Attendance at the conferences has increased over the years from about 100 in Paris in 1986 to 400 in Montreux (1998) except for the workshop in Ghana in 2000; this was the first in Africa for the HSC and it attracted a lesser number of participants (110) partly due to the longer distances, increased cost, increased time away from schools and apprehension on the part of some that Africa presented potential dangers from malaria and civil unrest. These conferences provide an important opportunity for Heads of IB schools to meet, for exchanges of information and ideas with IB staff, and for getting to know how IB programmes function in schools in different parts of the world.

In 2001 the HRC's name changed to the IHRC (International Heads Representative Committee) and this body was no longer directly elected by the Heads of IB schools. Instead, and for the first time (towards the end of 2000), Heads elected their own Regional Heads Representative Committees (RHRCs) of eight members each, voting only for candidates in their own region. The RHRCs correspond to the four IB regions: Africa/Europe/Middle East, Asia-Pacific, Latin America, North America and the Caribbean. Each RHRC then nominated four of its members to form the IHRC. Once formed, the IHRC elected its chair, vice-chair and secretary, and recommended four of its members – one from each of the RHRCs represented on the international committee – plus the chair of the IHRC to be members of the council of foundation. This still provides one third of the votes in the new council of foundation of 2001. This procedure ensures more equitable geographical representation on the IHRC and provides for more informed voting since Heads of schools are no longer asked to consider candidates worldwide. The HSC was renamed the Heads Standing Association (HSA) from 2003.

Notes

1. Lord (Robin) Hankey was the son of Lord (Maurice) Hankey, who was Secretary to the UK Imperial War Cabinet in the First World War and a minister in the War Cabinet 1939-40. Robin Hankey was a former ambassador both to Sweden and to the OECD, and a member of the first International Action Committee (founded in 1966 and developed into the United World Colleges International Committee) of Atlantic College. He took great interest in the IB project.

2. Those present were Charles Gellar (Copenhagen International School), Dick Irvine (Teheran IS), René-François Lejeune (International School of Geneva), David Sutcliffe (Atlantic College, Wales), Edgar Scherer (Lycée International St Germain en Laye, Paris), Yves le Pin (Ecole Nouvelle de Chailly, Switzerland) and the Heads of the following schools: Colegio Viaro (Barcelona), International School of Brussels, International School of London. Dan Wagner (Frankfurt IS) was to have attended but phoned at the conclusion of the meeting to say he was in London but could not find Peterson's office at West London College (Peterson 1976b).

3. As at 2010, these details can be updated as follows:

2003-2007: Tony Flatley, Collège Esther-Blondin, Quebec
2007-2009: Michael Matthews, Inter-Community School, Zurich
2009-: Sally Holloway, KIS International School, Thailand

In 2008 the IHRC became the Heads Council.

Part XI – Marketing the IB Diploma Programme to universities and schools

Introduction

The last chapter recounted how the creation of the HSC (1977) and the SCG (1978) provided the much-needed revenue for the IB to continue and assisted governance of the IB organization through representation on the IB's council of foundation.

This chapter relates to the period from 1963 to 1978. It attempts to demonstrate the considerable effort made to have the IB diploma known and recognised by many countries. During those years the ISES and then the IB office were involved in numerous marketing initiatives. Four main audiences were targeted:

- universities;
- schools;
- ministries of education and national governments; and
- examining bodies.

This chapter addresses the first two. The next will address the last two audiences.

It was crucial for university authorities to accept the proposed IB Diploma Programme otherwise the project would fail. Parents, students, teachers and school administrators needed to be convinced that the curricula were appropriate to international students and that they would be recognised by the best universities around the globe.

The most difficult marketing period was, of course, at the beginning when the IB was an unknown quantity and had yet to prove itself. By 1975 Heads, teachers, university admissions officers and government ministries were accepting the IB because of its proven success in a number of schools around the globe.

Two early publications helped to diffuse information, particularly to educational audiences, about the development of the as-yet fully untried IB: Martin Mayer's (1968) *Diploma: International Schools and University Entrance* and Robert Leach's (1969) *International Schools and Their Role in the Field of International Education.* Mayer's somewhat critical but objective approach complements Leach's more scholarly, idealistic one.

Some protagonists mentioned in this chapter have featured in previous instalments but readers may not remember who they are. The following information is therefore supplied.

Robert (Bob) Leach: commenced teaching history at the International School of Geneva in 1951; by 1960 he was head of history until his retirement in 1984. Seconded as an ISA consultant visiting schools around the world for one year (1961-62), he produced a report that recommended an 'international baccalaureate' for international school students. He produced the first IB course – contemporary world history – in 1963 and was a founding father of the IB programme.

Jean Siotis: professor (later director) of the Graduate Institute of International Studies and lecturer in international law at the University of Geneva; president of the first ISES examinations board in 1964, to officially become the IB examinations board in 1968.

Universities

Various initiatives took place in this regard with the objective of 'selling' the IB to universities. I have attempted to reconstruct the major activities, relying principally on a collection of documents, including reports of meetings, in a large folder entitled *ISES Files* housed in the archives of the IB in Geneva, on interviewees' recollections and on some primary and secondary sources of literature.

Peterson (1972, p34) identified five qualities that universities seek, or should seek, in prospective students:

- the ability to conceptualise and analyse;
- a sufficiently good memory for the student to be able to retain a number of facts or concepts in the mind simultaneously;
- 'unslaked curiosity';
- the ability to recognise (and more rarely to formulate) new interpretations of available information; and
- commitment to the intellectual formulation and solution of problems.

The reader will have noted that accumulating knowledge is not mentioned. Peterson saw this as 'obsolete' even in 1972; he stressed that learning how to learn was more important and would naturally develop from the above qualities. As a necessary complement to these intellectual capacities Peterson firmly believed in educating for humanity; he saw this as the indispensable other dimension of the educated individual. It was on this basis that he, with other IB staff and much external assistance, proceeded to convince universities to accept the IB diploma, at least for a trial period. He saw the IB Diploma Programme as the embodiment of the intellectual and humanitarian qualities that should be attractive to higher education institutions.

The first official action to convince universities was an ISES mission, headed by Cole-Baker, to the USA in March/April 1964 to introduce the IB idea. There was a very effective response from 'highly placed government, education and foundation officials' (Leach 1969, p50). Cole-Baker visited a number of universities and schools to bring about an awareness of the Geneva project. Between 1st and 15th April of the same year Leach and Siotis, president of the ISES examinations board, visited Harvard where the IB was favourably received (IB 1964). This university had already accepted a student who had completed the contemporary history examination in June 1963.

On 10 July 1964, an information meeting on the IB was given to the international conference of public instruction at the International School of Geneva. Various documents prepared by staff of the Geneva school were presented by Ruth Bonner (a former teacher at the school and then with ISES) and Gérard Renaud (teacher). Notable people present were Madame Bang (International Bureau of Education), Monsieur Delage (Senegal) and Monsieur Legrand (UNESCO). This assisted diffusion of the IB proposal amongst university educators (as well as schools and ministries). Teachers, who were closer to the needs of students than other actors, were playing an important role in the marketing of the IB. Moreover these were amongst the pioneers of IB curriculum development and their enthusiasm was infectious.

In January 1965 Renaud undertook an ISES mission to Paris where he spoke with officials of the French ministry of education, the director-general of Overseas Cooperation and the director-general of Cultural and Technical Affairs. As a result, acceptance of the IB in French universities was viewed favourably (Renaud 1965). At the same time Recteur Capelle of the French Education Ministry joined the ISES council; this was an important indication of interest by the French government.

In June 1965 the ISES council welcomed to its membership Harlan Hanson, director of the AP Program of the CEEB. He advised asking American colleges and universities to recognise the IB not for admission but for advanced placement. At the same time Desmond Cole, Head of UNIS, joined the ISES council. American support was now more manifest and official.

In July 1965, an important International Bureau of Education (IBE) conference was held in Geneva. The ISA delegate, Tom Carter (a language teacher at Atlantic College and member of the ISES IB modern languages curriculum committee), presented the IB. Interest was expressed from many countries. As a result of this IBE conference he suggested that a number of actions would assist IB development and acceptance. In October of the same year, Atlantic College members of the ISES executive were instrumental in gaining NATO parliamentary conference support for the IB in New York. This gave it status *vis-à-vis* American colleges (Leach 1969, p61).

Dr Hans Fischer-Wollpert, Head of a public school in Frankfurt, the Goethe Gymnasium, joined the ISES council in November 1965; he established the IB in influential German universities and education ministry circles (Leach 1969, p61).

There were now teachers, Heads and education officials engaged in promulgating the IB within a relatively short period of time.

February 1967 saw a landmark first IB conference at Sèvres at the invitation of the French ministry of education. Much activity had taken place from 1964 to 1966 in syllabus design and examination proposals.

> By the end of 1966 ... ISES was ready for the International Conference at Sèvres. ... What we hoped to achieve over the next year or two, as a result of the conference, was the agreement of enough universities, whether autonomous or controlled by their ministries of education, to cooperate in the experiment by giving at least provisional recognition to the IB as an entry qualification. (Peterson 2003, p30)

Education experts from the following countries, many of them university staff, were present: Belgium, Britain, Bulgaria, Cameroon, France, Federal Republic of Germany, India, Poland, Sweden, Switzerland, Tanzania, USA. Also present were representatives from CERN, which straddles Geneva and neighbouring France, Organization for Economic Cooperation and Development (OECD) in Paris, Oxford and Cambridge examining boards, Council of Europe in Strasbourg, Schools Council in London, and the European Economic Community in Brussels. The conference lasted three days and split into two groups. Commission A dealt with structure, standards, and syllabuses chaired by Dr Fischer-Wollpert with Renaud as consultant. Commission B discussed the organisation and procedures of the examination and was chaired by Robert Blackburn (deputy head of Atlantic College) with Dr Bill Halls (Department of Educational Studies, Oxford) as consultant. 'Seldom has a conference been as well-prepared and documented' (Leach 1969, p71). The conference made recommendations concerning the structure and standards of the IB. Negotiations for preliminary IB recognition by universities began at the colloquium and were to be continued as follows. In England, Canada, Switzerland and the USA each independent university was to be approached. In Belgium, France, the Netherlands and Italy it was necessary to contact the education ministry as universities in those countries were centrally controlled. In the Federal Republic of Germany, Scotland and Sweden approaches would be made to the single, academic authority (not the ministry of education) that controlled universities. At the conference Mr Hampton, director of CERN, offered to submit ISES syllabuses to his well-qualified experts who would then press governments to validate the exam amongst their 30 member nations. Such recognition by a prestigious international organisation was another positive step towards worldwide IB acceptance.

When the Ford Foundation grant was given, two consultants were appointed to the project in 1967: Dr Tyler and Dr Bowles, both education professionals. Tyler was also Professor of Education at the University of Chicago. Bowles had undertaken extensive research in 1963 for UNESCO on access to higher education, revealing divergences between national systems (Renaud 1975, p113). His support facilitated the 'selling' of the IB to reduce the difficulty of university access created by the different requirements around the world. Universities were attracted by practical considerations that would be in the self-interest of admissions officers. They were willing to participate in the six-year experiment (1970-1975) because the IB would reduce the difficult task of analysing and comparing many different national qualifications (Peterson 2003, p68).

In December 1967, the French and West German governments accorded university recognition to the IB except for their own nationals in their own countries. Fifteen universities in Britain – including Oxford, Cambridge and London – accepted the IB. In the USA, Harlan Hanson's College Board circular continued to recommend IB acceptance. McGill (Canada) and Australian and New Zealand universities accepted the IB together with the universities of Geneva, Zurich and St Gallen. Georges-Henri Martin, editor of the *Tribune de Genève* (a major newspaper), member of the board of the International School of Geneva and trustee of the Twentieth Century Foundation, assured recognition of the IB by the University of Geneva as he was also chairman of their academic council (IB 1990, p14). In the following years more universities were gradually added to the list through personal contacts by the IB directorate such as the 'Meeting of Experts on the Recognition of Diplomas in Higher Education in the Arab States', held in Beirut in December 1974 and attended by Renaud as IB deputy-director (IB 1975, p12).

Schools: teachers, students and parents

In January 1964, Eugene Wallach, teacher at the International School of Geneva, funded by a UNESCO grant, visited international schools in Teheran, Belgrade, Vienna, Milan, Brussels and the Hague to discuss the proposed IB. The IB was presented to participants at the European Teachers Association Conference, French Section (funded by the French government) at Sèvres. Oxford, Atlantic College and French ministry representatives were present. Because of the European Baccalaureate (whose first examination occurred in 1959) European Community schools supported the IB. The educational context of a supranational qualification, provided by the existence of the European Baccalaureate, assisted IB acceptance.

Cole-Baker (Head) and Miss McDowell (primary section) of the International School of Geneva visited international schools in some African countries in July 1964: Liberia, Ghana, Tanganyika (Moshi and Dar-es-Salaam). This led to ISA advisors being appointed to these schools and a greater awareness of the IB proposal. When Desmond Cole (Head) of UNIS joined the ISES council he assisted with the marketing of the IB in American schools. UNIS had wanted its own international diploma but saw the IB as the answer to their project and a programme that other schools could adopt to widen students' horizons.

Marketing of the IB idea to schools throughout the world was greatly facilitated by UNESCO through its Associated Schools Project contract, which commenced with the ISA in 1963 to study the problems of coordinating academic standards and curricula amongst international schools. Via its own communications system, UNESCO reached hundreds of schools around the globe (UNESCO 1964).

Martin Mayer, consultant to the 20th Century Fund, and Ruth Bonner, ISES executive secretary, made journeys to contact governments and schools in Europe during May and June 1965 (Leach 1969, p60). Mayer came with the Twentieth Century Fund grant to write a book and perform a technical analysis of the IB programme as it had developed so far.

From June to July of the same year Cole-Baker sent 16 teachers from his school to the USA and Canada to inform educators and schools of the IB and exchange ideas on international education. This was a very important mission from the International School of Geneva of teachers promulgating the IB. On 31 August 1965, Cole-Baker, Poirel and Renaud, of the International School of Geneva, met with John Sly of International Schools Services (ISS) in the USA to explain the IB. ISS had many member schools, particularly American schools overseas, and had been founded in 1955 initially as a North American off-shoot of ISA.

In 1967, Dr Tyler of the Ford Foundation said the IB was not only for international schools but that it should have an innovatory influence on national education systems (Renaud 1974, p5). This was eventually felt very much in the USA where currently about 90% of all IB schools are public institutions; the IB has had a positive influence on national curricula in a number of other countries. The current IB strategic plan encourages activities to assist national educational reform.

Like Mayer, Dr Tyler and Dr Bowles were, for funding reasons, acting as consultants to the IB project. At the second inter-governmental conference in London in 1978, mention was made of the positive effect the IB had had in 'internationalising' national education rather than being a special programme for a special group of students (IB 1978a, p2).

After the 1967 Sèvres conference, the desirability of developing a common curriculum, leading to examinations that would provide access to universities worldwide for internationally-mobile students, was not questioned. The concern was whether it was feasible. For this reason a six-year experiment (1970-1975) had been declared at the Sèvres conference and only highly reputable schools were admitted after careful negotiation. In addition to the International School of Geneva these included UNIS (New York), Atlantic College (Wales), J F Kennedy School (Berlin), International College (Beirut), Santiago College (Chile), the International Schools of Iranzamin (Iran) and Copenhagen, and two public institutions, the Goethe Gymnasium (Frankfurt) and the Lycée International de St Germain-en-Laye (Paris) (ISA 1968b). A number of these schools adopted the IB exclusively in 1968 or 1969.

Those involved agreed to the six-year experiment with different ideas in mind. Some members of the IB, particularly university staff like Professor Panchaud of the University of Geneva, 'initially conceived of the experiment as a piece of applied educational research' (Peterson 2003, p61). Ongoing technical analysis of the curricula, the examinations and the university performance of IB graduates was the main motivating factor. Others, notably Heads and education officials representing schools, saw the six-year experiment as the introductory phase of the permanent establishment of the IB. 'To them, any opportunities for pedagogical research, either in curriculum or examinations would be a minor spin-off' (Peterson 2003, p61). Heads generally were motivated by cultural, educational and ideological factors like Charles Sa'd of the National College, Choueifat, Beirut and member of the IB council, who was a 'great believer in education as a builder of bridges between communities, religions and nations' (Peterson 2003, p74).

A problem arose at the International School of Geneva when, in 1970, the board decided to replace all national examinations, except the Swiss *maturité*, by the IB. Competing interests led a certain number of parents to oppose this idea; they were worried about university acceptance of the IB for their children. The decision, however, stood, although no students sat for IB diplomas in 1970, only single subject certificates, and the opposition subsided when the students with IB diplomas in 1971 were easily admitted to British, French and American universities (Ecole International de Genève 1974, p276).

By 1975 a number of Heads, teachers, parents and students were attracted to the IB as a result of international diffusion: it had proven successful in an increasing number of schools across continents. This did not mean that the IB was accepted blindly; because IB diploma-holders were entering the best universities such as Harvard and Oxford it meant that the programme's content and standards were more attractive to interested schools – the IB was beginning to stand on its reputation. Ideological factors concerning intercultural understanding and the formation of world citizens played their part, but school Heads were also attracted by the academic rigour and content. International schools had been waiting for an appropriate international programme that would ensure worldwide university access.

The IB, already with a proven track record after five or six years, responded to the needs and it was beginning to spread. The only factor that sometimes prevented a school, particularly in a developing country, from adopting the IB was the cost of approximately 10,000 Swiss francs per annum, which was agreed when the HSC was founded in 1977.

Part XII – Marketing the IB Diploma Programme to ministries of education, government and examining bodies

Introduction

This discussion relates to the period from 1963 to 1978 during which the ISES and then the IB office were undertaking marketing initiatives. Four main audiences were targeted:

- universities
- schools
- ministries of education and national governments
- examining bodies.

The first two audiences were addressed in the last chapter. This chapter addresses the last two and includes the appearance, for the first time, of a geometrical representation of the IB Diploma Programme, an important marketing tool.

While the majority of schools at the time were independent, fee-paying schools, some were state-controlled institutions, which necessitated the agreement of education ministry officials before the IB could be implemented. This also applied to some countries where the education ministry controlled university education, for example in France (although this is no longer as true as it was). National pride plays an important role in the policies of governments, and this was no less true in gaining acceptance for an 'outside' qualification such as the IB Diploma Programme.

Contact with examination authorities was a delicate matter, because the IB could be seen as a threat to the quality of candidates presenting themselves for A levels, the French baccalaureate and AP examinations, for instance, by drawing the best students away from these national examinations offered both within the country and in British, French and American schools overseas. However, the contact proved fruitful and also provided considerable expertise when it came to examination procedures and the setting and marking of papers. This particular marketing action therefore assisted the quality of the IB examination process.

Ministries of education and governments

The approach to ministries of education and national governments was linked to programme development and delivery: education authorities were not only invited to accept IB students but to participate in the curriculum development and examination process by providing appropriate expertise. The consultants to the Ford Foundation, Dr Frank Bowles and Dr Ralph Tyler (both eminent educationists), emphasised at the time of the first Ford Foundation grant in 1966 that the project had potential beyond solving the problems of international schools. They saw the IB project as an opportunity for an exchange of educational ideas to assist national education reform. This was a major attraction to those educational reformers from state systems who gave much time to the project and facilitated the acceptance of the IB diploma by many governments.

In some countries education ministry approval was essential for university acceptance of the IB and for it to be trialled in government schools. Even where this was not the case, education ministry approval would give credibility to the IB in private, independent schools and to its recognition in universities. The French ministry of education was the first to be involved; its highly centralised tertiary and secondary education sectors made it mandatory to have ministerial blessing for trialling the IB in the state lycée at St Germain-en-Laye (Paris) and granting recognition in French universities. When ISES was formed it declared that English and French were to be the official languages for the IB examinations. This strengthened the support from the French ministry of education. In fact a French ISA committee chaired by Monsieur Trouillé was in existence in 1964 (ISA 1964).

Madame Hatinguais, Inspectrice Générale in the French ministry, was a member of the CIS and had been contacted by Leach about the IB through their connection as Quakers. She was a powerful figure in French education who, together with Recteur Jean Capelle, director of pedagogy with the French ministry of education and creator of the National Institute of Applied Sciences at Lyon, represented two distinguished leaders in educational reform in France. They both became very involved with ISES and the IB.

> The cooperation of the French reflects their sensitivity to significant programmes in education, and mirrors their appreciation of a bilingual English-French venture, by which an international clientele is offered relatively secure access to French universities and further appreciation of the culture they represent. (Leach 1969, p57).

In March 1964 French ministry officials were present at the French Section of the European Teachers Association (ETA) conference where the IB was presented. Renaud's visit in January 1965 to French ministry officials in Paris has already been mentioned for its importance in gaining university recognition of the IB in that country.

Mr Scherer, *proviseur* of the state-owned Lycée of St Germain-en-Laye near Paris was an advocate of the IB in his school. He took up his position there in

1965 (until 1989) as preliminary work on the IB was taking place in Geneva. Scherer was greatly impressed by the quality of those working for the IB. He first became involved in 1965 when an acquaintance introduced him to Dorothy Goodman in Paris, an American educator who founded Washington International School in 1966. She spoke to Scherer about the IB (Scherer 1992). From 1967 the IB office established exchanges with various international organisations (such as UNESCO's International Bureau of Education and the Council of Europe). In France, the IB office made contact with the Institut Pédagogique National, which led to its association with the Centre International d'Etudes Pédagogiques at Sèvres where Madame Hatinguais became director (Hayot 1984, p129). As a result, in 1969 the French government agreed to participate in a pilot project with the IB office for 15 years until 1984 and to accept the IB diploma as a university entrance qualification in France for foreign students studying in that country, and for French students studying abroad, but not for French nationals studying in France. At the time, the French education ministry was working on reforms to the French baccalaureate and it was believed that 'much of the support for the IB was due to the fact that the IB was very much on target in that it incorporated the commitment to general education while, at the same time, ensuring a great variety of choice, thus minimising early specialisation' (Hayot 1984, p130).

On the 14th and 15th of April 1964 Leach and Siotis, while on a mission to the USA to introduce ISES and the IB, were received by Jack Eager, assistant to U Thant (Secretary-General of the United Nations) in New York. He agreed to promote ISES and the IB project for the 'International Year of Development, 1965' – that is, to send information to all governments, UN associations, NGOs and branches of the UN in the Secretary-General's name (IB 1964). This was a most significant step in promulgating IB project information at the highest levels.

On the 3rd of May 1965, U Thant himself visited the International School of Geneva in connection with his undertaking to promote the IB project and for another reason. Picasso had donated a painting of his daughter for a UN stamp, which was to be sold to raise funds for the school and UNIS. U Thant was there to launch the stamp (Thomas 1992) as both schools had been originally created to educate the children of UN civil servants. Heads of school Meyer (Roquette had retired in 1964 after 33 years at the school) and Cole-Baker, together with the chairman of the board, Goormaghtigh, personally presented the IB proposal to U Thant on that occasion. His presence added a distinct mark of credibility to the acceptance of the IB diploma at government level in a number of countries.

On the 4th November 1964 Renaud presented the IB Diploma Programme to the 13th general session of UNESCO. This was supported by the Swiss and

Belgium delegations who asked the Director-General of UNESCO to recommend to the Secretary-General of the UN the inclusion of the IB project in the programme of the 'International Year of Development, 1965'. Leach and Siotis had paved the way in New York for the presentation by Renaud and the support of the Swiss and Belgium governments.

At the UNESCO annual conference in 1968, delegates representing Switzerland, Cameroon and Chile referred to the work of IB and its Oxford Research Unit and invited the Director-General of UNESCO to link the IB with the corresponding part of the UNESCO project on comparability, equivalence and recognition of diplomas (Renaud 1974, p7). The involvement of actors with such diplomatic leverage was positive for the IB. These representatives took this action because, in the context of UNESCO, the IB would help to redress the imbalance between developing and developed countries by providing a single accrediting agency for international standards. There was, however, still the problem of cost to the developing world. It is worth noting that two of the countries, Switzerland and Chile, each had a school participating in the six year experiment.

In 1968 IB was commissioned by CERN to provide a theoretical curriculum model for an international school to be set up on the site of its new accelerator (IB 1969). This showed great confidence in the IB from a very prestigious organisation with member governments scattered across the globe. In 1970, IB submitted to CERN in Geneva a paper entitled 'Design of a Theoretical Model for an International School at CERN II' (IB 1969). Hampton, director of CERN, wanted to attract the best researchers in the world so he had to provide appropriate international education for their children.

Influential members of the council of Atlantic College in Wales (founded in 1962) such as Lord Hankey were keen to create other colleges, first in Canada and Germany, and in so doing promoted the IB project both directly and indirectly with governments. In 1968 Lord Mountbatten[1] was elected chair of the Atlantic College council. The conditions of his acceptance were that the idea of the college should be spread to other countries and that an international office, which he would direct, should be set up. Propelled by ideology, he saw this 'as his final contribution to the avoidance of World War Three' (Peterson 2003, p66). He took Robert Blackburn as his Chief of Staff. Within a short time Mountbatten named the movement the United World Colleges (UWC) and he became president of its new international council for nine years until 1977.

During this period, with an international reputation that was legend in his own time, Mountbatten firmly rallied many influential people to the cause of IB and UWC: 'No head of state or minister of education, cornered at a government reception or private dinner party, had much chance of escape.' (Peterson 2003, p106). Peterson had served on Mountbatten's staff in South-East Asia during the

Second World War, so the first director general of the IB office, who had taken such an interest in Atlantic College, was very well supported by the first president of the UWC movement. 'Lord Mountbatten came often to the British Embassy in Paris and met with French government ministers to promote the IB.' (Scherer 1992). Mountbatten perceived the potential of the IB. He travelled around the world calling on his many contacts to promote UWCs and the IB.

He went to Geneva in 1971 to present the first diplomas awarded to students at the school. Georges-Henri Martin, member of the board of the International School of Geneva and editor of the *Tribune de Genève*, received him on behalf of the city and the international school and exclaimed: '*Le jour viendra où Genève sera fière d'avoir été le berceau de deux grandes idées généreuses – la Croix-Rouge et le Baccalauréat International.*' [The day will come when the city of Geneva will be proud to have been the birthplace of two great and noble ideas – the Red Cross and the International Baccalaureate.] (Renaud 2001a). This provided excellent publicity for the IB in Switzerland and abroad.

In 1970, International Education Year, 'IBO sent full information on all activities to education ministers of all member states of the UN, encouraging them to give their support to this international experiment' (IB 1970a, p17). The annual ISA conference was held at UN Headquarters, New York, where U Thant gave the opening address.

In 1972 Peterson addressed a number of meetings on the IB in the UK including the annual conference of Her Majesty's Inspectors. He spoke on BBC radio about his book, which was published in the same year by Harrap: *International Baccalaureate: an experiment in international education* (IB 1972a, p11).

In May 1974 Goormaghtigh, chair of the IB council of foundation, attended a meeting of ministries of education in Europe held in Bucharest; solutions to student mobility, the content and duration of higher education and new trends in curricula and methods were among the issues discussed. This provided very useful contacts for the IB *vis-à-vis* European universities (IB 1975, p13).

In 1974 Peterson and Renaud, director and deputy-director of the IB respectively, attended the 18th general conference of UNESCO and sought to establish the IB under UN control from 1977 for economic reasons (Peterson 1972, p31). As has been recounted elsewhere in this series, this was not to be.

At the second inter-governmental IB conference in London in February 1978, the Secretary of State for Education and Science, Shirley Williams, spoke of the flexibility and choice provided by the IB and the need to rethink English A levels as a result. This was a politically powerful message in support of the IB.

Examining bodies

Contact with the French ministry of education had also provided direct links with those responsible for the French baccalaureate examination. Where an education system was highly centralised, as in France, the task of promulgating the IB to the various educational layers – universities, examining boards and schools – was much less onerous on the ISES and the IB office. A major drawback would occur, however, if the central authority rejected the idea; in this case its educational constituents must comply. (The reverse is, of course, equally true). This could mean, for instance, that the French baccalaureate examining board would not permit the IB to be taught in French government schools and would not recognise the IB for university entrance in France, even where the IB had been obtained in a school in another country.

A decentralised system, while requiring much more effort and expense to contact all relevant authorities, is able to accommodate different responses at different levels. For example, an education ministry in one state in Germany or Australia might not accept the IB to be taught in government schools, yet the universities in the same state might readily agree to accept IB diploma-holders from other states or countries. The independent components of a decentralised system reduce the possibility of total rejection but create a more complex and expensive marketing exercise. In a highly centralised system, the relevant authority, once it agrees, will ensure compliance through its own communication networks. The French baccalaureate examining board was, then, very interested as the French education ministry had accepted the idea in principle.

Education in the USA, while highly decentralised in many respects, did (and still does) have one recognised authority for college and university entrance examinations: the CEEB. When Dr Harlan Hanson, director of the AP Program of the CEEB, joined the ISES council in January 1965 the support of his examination board followed. The CEEB did not, however, control the colleges and universities; it provided a service across the USA that was accepted by the tertiary institutions. The CEEB suggested to its constituency that the IB be accepted for AP and the colleges and universities agreed.

The February 1967 Sèvres IB conference was a landmark in bringing together four education officials representing examining boards from different countries.

For the first time in history the director of the College Entrance Examination Board, the director of the French baccalaureate, the director of the Oxford-Cambridge Examination Board and the director of the Swiss Federal Maturité sat down to discuss educational matters together (Leach 1969, p70).

The examining boards reached agreement to support the IB: these actors recommended trial examinations and provided expert examiners to ensure that the IB fulfilled national requirements. They were influenced by technical analysis of the programme, which revealed academic rigour, an innovative pedagogical approach, and a rich diversity of student evaluation methods. They saw the potential to improve their own national systems by being involved in the pooling of ideas on an international scale.

The IB Diploma Programme hexagon

The visual representation of the IB Diploma Programme became an important marketing tool some time after the earlier exercises described above to gain recognition for the new international curriculum and examination. This occurred in the form of a hexagon (which is still used today) and it set the example for the later geometrical representation of the Middle Years Programme (MYP) as an octagon and the Primary Years Programme (PYP) as a hexagon.

The Diploma Programme was first depicted as a hexagon by Professor Jeff Thompson, at the time chief examiner for chemistry and the physical sciences. It occurred during a conference of the *Fondazione Cine* in Venice, 9-11 December 1983, where he spoke about the IB Diploma Programme and presented it on an overhead projector transparency (Renaud 2001b). Jeff is well known for his propensity to visualise ideas. His geometrical shape corresponded to the six groups of subjects with the extended essay, ToK and CASS (creative and aesthetic activity, and social service), as it was at the time, in the middle. CASS became CAS (creativity, action, service) in 1989.

Renaud had been present at the meeting in Venice and liked the visual representation. In a paper on the ToK, Renaud (1986) refers to the way in which Thompson's schema showed the coherence of the IB Diploma Programme through the hexagonal structure. Renaud saw the ToK as the centre piece. He then went on to say how better it would be if the figure became three-dimensional with the hexagon at the base of a pyramid and the ToK at the peak. The base and sides give volume to the pyramid in the same way that, from the disciplines at the base, the pyramid draws its volume culminating in the ToK at the summit. This interesting idea was never implemented.

Thompson used the hexagon again at a major IB conference at the University of London in 1988 (Hayden *et al* 1995, pp131-2). However, it was not until 1993 that the hexagonal representation of the IB Diploma Programme first appeared officially in IB documents, notably in a number of subject guides printed that year.

Notes

1. Mountbatten was killed in 1979 by an IRA bomb planted in his boat as he was fishing with his family off the coast of Ireland. He was 79 years of age.

126

Part XIII – Expansion of IB offices

Introduction

The office in Geneva was and remains the headquarters of the IB organization, but from the very beginning there was a presence in the UK that became more important as the years went by. This began with Alec Peterson in 1966, whose changing geographical location in the UK as director of the ISES and then director general of the IB office (as it was originally called) was outlined in Part VI. The changing locations of the examinations office (gradually expanded to include other functions), and the research unit in Oxford are discussed.

Examinations office

Initially the IB Diploma Programme examinations administration was done in the Geneva office. As the number of schools grew it became clear that more space and personnel would be necessary. While it was politically and symbolically correct to have the headquarters of the IB in Geneva, where many international organisations had settled, it was an expensive city. Peterson argued strongly for decentralisation of the examination administration to the UK because:

- it would grow quickly and cost too much in Geneva;
- the majority of schools worked in English and it was more difficult to recruit English-speaking staff in an international French-speaking city. (Peterson 2003, p186).

Tom Carter had been head of languages at Atlantic College and an enthusiastic supporter of the IB project. He was then appointed director of the Language Centre at Southampton University. Research into language teaching and examining was one of the centre's main functions and Peterson wanted to make use of this expertise for the IB. Initially the centre provided batteries of tests in different languages for the IB. Then in 1974 the IB entered into a contract with the university for additional space so that the preparation and administration of all IB language examinations could take place there under the direction of Dianne Williamson (who arrived at the centre in 1975) with overall assistance from Tom Carter.

Until 1980 Ruth Bonner had been in charge of IB examination administration in Geneva (except for the IB language examinations) but she retired in that year and Marion Strudwick was appointed director of IB examinations at the Southampton Language Centre, now employing five people. This signified the decision to transfer all of the IB's examination administration to the UK.

But there were some computer problems and the IB decided to wait for the delivery of the new computer service in 1981 before transferring the whole examination section to the UK (IB 1980, p12). So, in 1981 all IB examinations, except for languages, were administered from a new location at the Institute of Education, London University, where Peterson had been in 1976-77 followed by Blackburn in 1978 as deputy director general of the IB organization. The director general, Gérard Renaud, was full time in Geneva from 1977. The IB language examinations continued to be administered from Southampton until 1983. Marion Strudwick and most of her staff had moved in 1981 to London University; she was replaced by Derek Goulden in 1982.

As the number of candidates grew, larger space was again needed and a decision was made to move the IB's complete examination administration to the University of Bath in 1984. Colin Jenkins became director of examinations in 1987, replacing Goulden, and spent the 1987-88 year in Bath. The examinations office occupied a top floor corridor in the Department of Education at the University of Bath. In 1986 there were 21 people in that corridor (three of whom had computers) and two more in the computer department, which was housed in the basement of a separate building. The five computers were linked to the mainframe computer of Bath University. In 1988 the IB organization bought its first mainframe computer while still in Bath; it was huge and underpowered by today's standards. The data preparation of examination entries (received on paper from schools) was done off site in the south of England and the computer tape was sent by courier to Bath.

During its time at Bath, the IB examinations office made a number of important innovations, capitalizing on its location within a university environment. This included the creation of the Assessment Research and Development Advisory Committee (ARDAC) consisting of the director of examinations, the chair of the examining board and a research officer. This committee oversaw assessment research and later broadened this to include a wider curriculum dimension. The committee ceased to exist in 1990.

The approach to IB examinations was to encourage and reward responses that reflected critical thinking skills. Peterson had shown interest in a range of assessment techniques that would gauge 'the whole endowment and personality of the student' (Peterson 1987, p50) and which complemented his ideas on curriculum development. His concept of student evaluation, developed over a number of years, formed part of a study he did for the Council of Europe in 1970. He did not want good teaching to be distorted by intensive examination preparation. He thought highly of oral examinations with a visiting examiner (a hallmark of IB language A, now A1, examinations for many years), of mixing a small amount of multiple choice testing in some subjects with essays, of assessing analytical skills and cultural sensitivity rather than factual recall, of qualitative measures of affective development (identified particularly through CAS in the IB Diploma Programme). These are still the ideas underpinning the philosophy of student assessment in the IB.

Expansion of IB organization functions in the UK and the emergence of IBCA
Since computer technology was so important for examination administration, staff were recruited to maintain and update this sector and a finance department was also created at Bath, in addition to the finance department in Geneva. Tony Martell was finance and administration manager from 1987. The IB office in Bath moved to St Mellons technology park near Cardiff in 1989. "We took over a cavernous warehouse and in the space of ten weeks converted it into an elegant office," said Colin Jenkins, the director of examinations at the time. (IB 1989, p5) Tony Martell played a key role in securing the new property at Cardiff and oversaw the considerable logistics involved in the move in 1989, including that of a huge mainframe computer. He died in February 1993 following a six month struggle with cancer.

A new director of examinations, Clive Carthew, was appointed from 1990 at the new rented premises in St Mellons, called IBEX (IB Examinations). IBEX was in fact a misnomer as the Cardiff office was vitally involved in curriculum development for the Diploma Programme, and not just examinations. In 1991 the IB organization's annual report mentioned that more emphasis was to be given to systematic curriculum development (for the diploma) and a curriculum support team was established from January 1992.

The 'cavernous warehouse' soon became too small and in 1993 the IB rented a sister building across the street in St Mellons. At that point the two companion spaces became known as the Green Building and the Red Building.

By 1994 there were 545 diploma schools (from 313 in 1986) and the rented premises at St Mellons were no longer adequate to house the increasing staff and the examination scripts, so a search for another location was underway. In 1995 Andrew Bollington (who had been with the IB computer section since 1991) was appointed IT manager; this was in response to the growing need for information technology support.

In January 1996 a new, much larger building, still in St Mellons and just a short distance from the rented premises, was purchased. This was the first piece of real estate to be owned by the IB organization. It was a two-storey building of 2232 square metres in a technology park and 124 staff occupied it when the IB moved in. Andrew spent much time crawling around the floor to install computer cabling in the two months that preceded the move to the new premises in April 1996. HRH Princess Sarvath El Hassan of Jordan officially opened the building in October 1996 and named it Peterson House after Alec Peterson, the first director general of the IB Organization.

During 1994 the Cardiff office ceased to be called the examinations office and adopted a title much more in keeping with the work it had been doing for many years and which was soon to be enhanced by the MYP and PYP, where no external examinations apply. It became the curriculum and assessment office or IBCA for short. The office in Cardiff had always been the base for curriculum development, student assessment techniques, examinations, financial management, computing, information technology and publications just like its predecessor in Bath. The increasing importance of ICT support was marked by Andrew Bollington's appointment as head of ICT in 2000 and then as the first director of ICT in 2003.

Two major divisions – academic affairs, and business and finance – were established in the Cardiff office in 1997. A new director of academic affairs, Helen Drennen, was appointed in the same year and a new title of director of business and finance with increased responsibilities was given to an existing senior staff member, Stuart Chapman.

In 1999, when Peterson House was no longer adequate, further space was rented in an adjacent building, and acquiring more space became a priority in early 2000. By the end of 2000 the IB organization had arranged to rent new premises under construction in Cardiff Bay. So the Cardiff office moved again in April 2001. The name Peterson House was retained for the new building. The assistant director general of education for UNESCO, Sir John Daniel (formerly Vice Chancellor of the Open University in the UK and vice-president of the IB council of foundation 1996-99), performed the official opening in November 2001.

A translation unit was created in 1997 to oversee all translation work. Six people who are native speakers of either French or Spanish were employed full time in 2001. In 2007 there were 13 staff in the Languages Services Department (renamed September 2004), including a translator for Chinese from May 2002. They oversee the translation of subject guides in all programmes, of examination papers, promotional literature, other IB publications and some of the IB website material; they check for consistency in the use of IB terminology. This department has added a considerable degree of professionalism to the translation work of the IB.

Today the examinations office and the ICT division are part of the IB's new, large three-storey building of 5000 square metres in the Cardiff Gate Business Park and occupied by 260 staff (in 2007). It also houses an academic directorate (curriculum development and student assessment for all three programmes), business and finance, human resources, translation and publications. IB Diploma Programme schools have been registering examination candidates electronically since 1994.

130

In 2006 the IB organization leased further premises of 15,000 square feet at East Gate, near Cardiff to store all IB Diploma Programme examination scripts. Seven staff work in that building with a seasonal augmentation of around 300 script checkers during late May and June each year.

Oxford and Bath Research Units

As previously noted, this unit was set up, initially under the direction of Dr Bill Halls, at the Department of Educational Studies, Oxford University, in 1967 and it closed in 1974. Mr Leslie Stephens was appointed in 1969 (during his retirement) to the position of university liaison officer for the UK, working from Eastbourne, Sussex. He worked very effectively to gain recognition of the IB Diploma by universities in the UK. From 1972-74 he was attached to the Research Unit but did not change residence to live in Oxford.

Dr Kevin Marjoribanks, a visiting academic from South Australia, took over the direction of the unit from September 1972 until it closed in 1974. This unit analyzed IB examination results, compared them with national examination results, followed up students at university, and contributed to the development of curricula and assessment techniques.

It took 12 years before it was decided to re-establish an explicit research function within the organization. In 1986 Derek Goulden (the then director of the IB examinations office, based in the University of Bath) appointed Mary Hayden (previously subject officer for IB mathematics and science) as research and development officer, a post she held until 1991, after the move of the office to St Mellons in Wales. In 2000, an IB research unit was established at the University of Bath and it became operational under the direction of Professor Jeff Thompson. Jeff has had a very long association with the IB.

In 1968 Jeff, in collaboration with Bill Halls of the Department of Educational Studies, University of Oxford, was undertaking a study for the Council of Europe on the teaching of chemistry across 19 European countries. At the time Jeff was a researcher in chemistry at University College London and was on secondment from Watford Grammar School where George Walker (director general of the IB organization 1999-2005) was a member of Jeff's chemistry department. Alec Peterson knew about Jeff because of the Council of Europe study and rang him in 1968 with a request to provide some multiple choice questions for the trial examinations in IB chemistry, which he did. Alec then said, a little later, that his department had a vacancy to train chemistry teachers and asked Jeff to join them.

Jeff was also concurrently appointed to Keble College, Oxford, as a lecturer in physical organic chemistry and at the same time trained chemistry teachers and researched in Alec's department. He subsequently became director of

131

postgraduate education and acting director of the department. Jeff took up a chair of education at the University of Bath in 1979 which he held until his retirement at the end of 2005. His association with the university continues as Emeritus Professor.

He was chief examiner in chemistry and in physical science for the IB, coordinator for group 4 subjects (the experimental sciences), and chair of the bureau and examining board from 1984 until 1989. He also presided over curriculum committees for the introduction of environmental systems and design technology. He was a member of the original curriculum board, the executive committee and the council of foundation. Jeff was founding director of the Centre for the study of Education in an International Context (CEIC), which he established in 1991 at the University of Bath. Dr Mary Hayden became director of the CEIC in 2000. Jeff was also founding editor of the *Journal of Research in International Education*, which was first published in 2002 with assistance from the IB organization. Mary Hayden became editor-in-chief of the journal in 2006.

Jeff chaired the IB research committee, which was established in November 1998. From January 2000 Jeff became an IB staff member as director of international education, based in Bath with responsibility for the new IB research unit, which he established in the same year in the same location. In 2007 there were six people employed in this research division of the IB. Jeff stepped in to fill a vacancy as academic director from September 2002 until October 2003 in Cardiff. Subsequently he resumed IB duties in Bath as head of the IB research unit until his retirement at the end of 2005.

Part XIV – IB regional offices

Introduction

The growth of the IB regional offices is the focus of this chapter . Regional offices are the 'shop front' for the IB. It is the regional office staff who are eyeball-to-eyeball with the school personnel via the increasing number of workshops and conferences, and authorization and programme evaluation visits.

IB World Schools are the 'shop front' for international education. We often hear that we are not sure what international education is, but the IB network of schools represents tangible evidence of this phenomenon ... and they were all shepherded in by regional offices.

So I hope you enjoy the brief stories of the emergence of IB regional offices in London, New York, Buenos Aires, Singapore and Geneva.

Regional offices

The main tasks of the regional offices are to:

- disseminate information about IB programmes to interested schools;
- conduct the authorisation process for schools wishing to offer an IB programme, including a visit to the schools and a subsequent report to the director general;
- administer a comprehensive annual teacher training programme of workshops and conferences to support all three IB programmes;
- attend to issues of recognition for the Diploma and to a lesser extent the MYP *vis-à-vis* universities, ministries of education or other awarding bodies;
- monitor the quality of the three programmes after authorisation; and
- promote IB programmes within the region.

The following annual quality assurance procedures for the IB Diploma Programme had been operating for some time through the regional offices:

- unscheduled visits to schools on examination administration;
- random sampling of student CAS records;
- perusal of examination results and contacting schools with particularly poor results; and
- identification of schools not regularly sending teachers to IB workshops and conferences.

An important additional measure was introduced in 1996 by IBNA (the North American regional office); this was a questionnaire to be sent to 20% of diploma schools each year, which had had the programme for at least five years, and was called 'The Five Year Programme Review'. It enquired into programme implementation, maintenance and future expansion within the school.

The IBNA questionnaire was then used in an adapted form in other regions; the responses were analysed by the IB regional offices and feedback was given to the school with commendations and recommendations. This was repeated every five years for each school.

As a quality assurance mechanism, the Primary Years Programme (PYP), offered from 1997, and the Middle Years Programme (MYP), offered from 1994, have a compulsory evaluation visit three and four years respectively after authorisation, then every five years thereafter. Where possible, joint programme evaluation visits for these programmes are undertaken with ECIS (European Council of International Schools) accreditation visits, in order to avoid duplication of effort for MYP or PYP schools that are also ECIS members. The possibility of partnering with other school accreditation agencies is also envisaged.

From 2005 the same system of programme evaluation was introduced for the three programmes whereby schools complete a self-study followed by a school visit (for the MYP and PYP only). The 'Five Year Programme Review' has been superseded by quite an elaborate self-study questionnaire, which is identical for all programmes with the addition of separate appendices pertaining to particularities of each programme. Unlike the MYP and PYP, the IB organization has not had the resources to date to undertake on-site visits for the many and growing IB Diploma Programme evaluations that take place each year; a visit is organized only in those cases where the self-study is showing signs of trouble.

IBNA was the first regional office and it was established in 1975. The year 1978 is significant because it marks the appointment of, for the first time, four part-time IB representatives in countries other than Switzerland, the UK and the USA where IB offices were already located. Two of these representatives were in the Asia-Pacific region (in Australia and the Philippines), one was in France and one in Uruguay. From these modest beginnings the other three regional offices emerged.

The importance of the regions was recognised when, in 1990, those in charge ceased to be called 'regional officers' and were given the title 'regional directors'. The IBNA office had a regional board from 1976. The other three regions did not have a board but they each have, since 2001, a regional advisory committee of 11 members that meets twice a year to interact with the regional director. From 2007 these are now called 'regional council' with the same advisory role.

In terms of staffing (2007 figures) IBNA is the largest office (42 full time staff), IBAEM the second (30), IBAP the third (24), and IBLA the fourth (19).

This order has remained unchanged for many years and corresponds to the number of authorised IB programmes (a number of schools teach more than one programme) in each region. The table below indicates the number of programmes per region in January 2008:

	DP	MYP	PYP	Total programmes
IBNA	699	344	164	1207
IBAEM	546	105	98	749
IBAP	216	105	108	429
IBLA	194	44	54	292

The development of each regional office from its beginnings is now discussed.

IB North America

Some American Heads were members of the Conference of Internationally-minded Schools from 1949 and of the ISA, which was formed in 1951, comprising mainly parents in its early years. Miss Julia Henderson, a parent at UNIS, New York, was on the ISA committee in 1961 and some UNIS teachers had been involved in the Conference of Teachers of Social Studies in International Schools held at the International School of Geneva in 1962, when ideas about an international qualification for university entrance were discussed.

Forbes went from the International School of Geneva (where he was head of the English Language Section from 1956-1961) as Head of UNIS in 1961-1962 and was succeeded by Desmond Cole who became Headmaster of UNIS in the following year. Cole was a member of the IB council of foundation in Geneva from 1969-74. Hence knowledge about the evolution of the IB started with UNIS in the USA. In addition many IB marketing missions took place to universities and schools in North America from 1962 to 1970 with assistance from Dr Harlan Hanson (director, AP Program, CEEB).

As a result of growing IB interest in the USA and Canada (UNIS was a trial examination school from 1967), and the implementation of the IB in a rapidly growing number of schools in that part of the world from 1970, the need for a North American IB office began to emerge. In the 1973-74 school year, Peterson was at UNIS to promote the IB and at the UN Staff Association, UN

Headquarters. Members of the Hegeler Foundation were present at the latter *exposé* and agreed to provide US$15,000 to set up a North American committee for the IB.

This eventuated in 1975 with Desmond Cole (Head of UNIS) as chair and Harlan Hanson as secretary (IB 1973a). Hanson became involved because he saw an educationally interesting problem (university access for international students), which the IB had the potential to solve and which would provide an international education at the same time (Hanson 1992). He remained on the IBNA board from 1976-90 and was a member of the first IB council of foundation in Geneva from 1967-76. The objectives of the North American committee were to:

- provide information on the IB for North America;
- consult with schools and colleges regarding the IB programme;
- select American teachers to join IB examiner teams; and
- arrange American participation in IB curriculum development.
  (IB 1973a)

The formation of IBNA and the promulgation of the IB in that part of the world owes much to Blouke Carus. As CEO of Open Court publishing house he had a strong commitment to lifting academic standards in American schools and had sponsored conferences on educational reform at which eminent educators spoke. The papers delivered were published in a regular series. Blouke had read about the IB in the *International Herald Tribune* and was quick to seize its potential for assisting education in national American schools; he also saw the need for an effective promotion campaign.

Blouke helped organize, with Alec Peterson, the meeting at UNIS in December 1973 to present the IB to North American educators. At the conclusion of that meeting the idea crystallized to form a separate board to raise money and to promote the IB in North America. It was Blouke who negotiated the first grant from the Hegeler Institute of which he was a trustee; he became the chair of the IBNA board when it was officially constituted in 1977 and remained in that capacity until 1989.

Blouke wanted to devote more time to the IB council of foundation, which he had joined in 1977 (and remained a member until 1993). In order to do this and remain active with the IBNA board, a position of president of the board, co-terminus with that of the chair, was created from 1980. Tom Hagoort became president of the IBNA board from 1980 until 1991. So, during nine years (from 1980 until 1989) the board had both a president and a chair.

From 1990 the position of chair was abolished. Tom Hagoort was an international lawyer who had assisted the relocation of UNIS in New York and the founding of the Washington International School by Dorothy Goodman (a member of the North American Committee for the IB in 1975 and then an IBNA board member from 1976 until 1987). Hagoort was a member of the IB council of foundation from 1983, and president from 1990 until 1996.

The chairs, then presidents, of the IBNA board from the past to the present are as follows:[1]

1975-1977: Desmond Cole, chair (of the North American committee for the IB)
1977-1989: Blouke Carus, chair
1980-1991: Thomas Hagoort, president
1991-1993: Anthony Macoun, president
1993-2002: Robert Pearmain, president
2002-2005: Evelyn Levsky Hiatt, president
2005-: Delia Pompa, president

At the time of their presidencies, Tony Macoun was Head of the Lester B Pearson United World College of the Pacific, Vancouver, and Bob Pearmain was former associate superintendent with the Vancouver School Board in British Columbia; prior to that, he had been Head of Sir Winston Churchill Secondary School. Ms Hiatt retired in 2002 after working for the Texas Education Agency for 25 years as senior director for Advanced Academic Services. Ms Pompa was former director of the Office of Bilingual Education and Minority Languages Affairs in the US Department of Education.

IBNA is the only regional office to have a board with its own official statutes. This came about because the office needed funds to operate and the IB organization in Geneva had no funds in the mid 1970s to establish and maintain an office in New York. There were a number of North American foundations willing to provide such support for the benefit of American education but they were not prepared to channel funds into an international organization in Geneva, for which, in addition, they would have had no tax relief. There was also the difficulty of schools, particularly state institutions, paying annual fees to a body outside North America.

Over the launching years of IBNA total contributions were received from other benevolent foundations as follows:

Andrew W Mellon Foundation US$330,000
Exxon Education Foundation US$100,000
Geraldine Dodge Foundation US$85,000

Some corporate donors also contributed small amounts of approximately US$1000 over a number of years: Dresdner Bank, *New York Times* Foundation and Western Electric. Interest in Canada also brought grants of approximately US$10,000 from Gulf Canada and Imperial Oil (Peterson 2003, p149).

So the IBNA office and IBNA board were created. Financially IBNA collected IB school subscriptions, keeping one fifth and sending four fifths to Geneva. With the grants mentioned above and the rapid increase in schools in North America, IBNA was able to be financially solvent.

The executive director for the first year (1976-77) was Dr Charles Rose, an art historian (non-education professional). He was succeeded in August 1977 by Gilbert Nicol who continued until 1986. He had a legal background, had spent a number of years in college and university administration (university staff) and was committed to the IB. Nancy Weller was appointed regional officer from 1986 and regional director from 1990.

Before joining the IB in 1984, she worked as communications director for two Geneva-based international organizations. In addition to print journalism, she was involved in religious and cultural affairs programming for Canadian and US television networks. Nancy held a BA from Wellesley College in Massachusetts and a Master's in psychology and religious studies from the University of Chicago.

During the 1992-93 school year, Nancy became involved in some communications work for the whole IB organization and the first issue of *IB World* was produced under her editorship (from 1992-98), appearing three times a year. Ellen Wallace was editor from 1999-2004; she introduced a lighter recycled paper and reduced size version without the glossy cover from 2001, appearing four times a year. Mary Hayden was editor for the four 2005 issues of the magazine. In 2006 Ann Oliver became editor of *IB World* and introduced a slightly smaller format and a new style. It presents a professional kaleidoscope that includes news, views, curriculum and assessment issues, CAS projects, and teacher workshops calendars.

In September 1994 Nancy Weller became director of communication in the Geneva head office and Bradley Richardson (who had been deputy regional director) was appointed regional director of IBNA, a post he still occupied until leaving the organization at the end of 2007, marking 22 years of service. Before he joined the IB in 1985, Brad was an assistant professor of English at Atlantic Union College in Massachusetts. He also taught English at Loma Linda University in California, where he coordinated the university's freshman English composition program. He holds a bachelor's degree and a Master's degree from Loma Linda University.

Most IBNA schools are public, government institutions where the IB was accepted because of its:

- academic rigour;
- potential to upgrade and enrich national school curricula;
- international perspective;
- integrated structure of studies;
- motivating effect on teachers and students; and
- facilitation of internal US (as well as international) mobility.

Some schools hesitated about adopting the IB because of:

- high cost;
- lack of recognition of the quality by some universities;
- complicated administration procedures;
- heavy workload for students; and
- communication difficulties with Geneva.

(Fox 1985, p64).

Except for the cost, the other problems diminished as IBNA expanded.

In 1987 the New York office undertook an improved procedure for evaluating schools seeking IB authorisation, whereby a team of three visited schools prior to the authorisation visits themselves. For the first time, in the same year, a document about IB diploma recognition policies of North American universities was compiled. 1992 saw the beginning of a joint publishing venture of the best IB history extended essays in the *Concord Review*, an academic, history periodical.

There has been continued growth of state, regional and provincial coalitions of IB schools; 24 sub-regional IB schools associations were active in 2008. These groups have assisted the promulgation of information about the IB diploma and the work of the regional office in maintaining and improving university recognition. Many of the school associations now provide teacher training workshops officially outsourced by the IBNA office for an ever increasing number of participants.

In September 1994 the first MYP manager for a regional office was appointed in the person of Maggie Maguire and the first MYP teacher training workshops were held in March and June 1995 in Denver and at the UWC of the American West in Montezuma, New Mexico. Some 27 schools in Quebec had been doing the MYP as the former ISA curriculum since the late 1980s. The ministry of education had taken up the ISA curriculum and implemented it in French in 27 state schools belonging to the *Société des Ecoles d'Education Internationale* (Society of Schools of International Education).[2] All of these schools have since been authorised as IB MYP schools.

In 1994 the IBNA office in New York also assumed responsibility for the Caribbean region.

During the 1994-95 year Minnesota and Texas joined Florida and Georgia to reimburse public schools participating in IB teacher training and subsidies for students to do the IB diploma. By 1998, IBNA had influenced state education departments to pay more than US$12 million per year in the USA to assist IB schools and students for all three IB programmes. Similar initiatives continue to take place since that time. The IBNA regional office operates in English and French.

IB Africa, Europe, Middle East (IBAEM)

The Mission Laïque Française is a private organization founded in 1902 in Paris. Its major objective is to spread French language and culture around the world via a pedagogy that emphasises intercultural understanding and non-sectarian teaching. It has over 70 private schools (these are not the French *lycées* overseas) in countries other than France.

During the 1970s a number of high ranking public servants in the French ministry of education and associated educational institutions were very active in the development of the IB Diploma Programme. This led to the Mission Laïque Française, which had shown interest in the IB development in Geneva, becoming an official representative of the IB organization in France from 1978 until 1981, when the IB fell out of favour with the ideals of the new socialist government providing support to that organization.

The IB organization was seen as an elitist institution providing an educational programme for students from rich families on the international circuit in expensive, private schools. (Today about 50% of all IB World Schools are public or state with no tuition fees and about 65% of all IB diploma examination candidates are from public schools.)

Robert Blackburn joined the IB organization from Lord Mountbatten's UWC international office in 1978 as director of development and deputy director general. He moved into the IB office at the University of London's Institute of Education, which had been occupied by Peterson during the last two years before his retirement. In 1984 this London location also became a regional office for Europe with Blackburn in charge.

From July 1986 responsibility for Europe moved to Geneva, where Monica Flodman, as regional officer (director from 1990), established a European regional office and Blackburn's London location became the first regional office for Africa and the Middle East. In 1987 Philippa Leggate, head of the American-British Academy, Muscat, Oman, was appointed part-time representative for the Middle East to assist the London office.

Robert Blackburn died of a heart attack in 1990. The London office then closed and Geneva headquarters dealt with Africa and the Middle East until September

1991, when Philippa Leggate was appointed full time regional director for Africa and the Middle East operating from the IB's Cardiff premises. She was also appointed director for the UK within the European office, which operated from Geneva (IB 1991, item 4.1). Tony Macoun took over from Philippa in August 1993. Tony came from his post as Head of the UWC in Vancouver and had an additional role as director of development. In October 1993, Monica Flodman moved to open a sub-regional office in Stockholm with specific responsibilities for the Nordic countries and Central/Eastern Europe and Ian Hill was appointed regional director for Europe in Geneva. The regional office for Africa and the Middle East in Cardiff closed in July 1994 (when Tony took up a post as founding Head of the new UWC in Norway) and it amalgamated with Europe to form the Africa/Europe/Middle East regional office in Geneva. Part-time regional advisors were established in Jordan and Kenya in 1995.

Nélida Antuña-Baragaño (from Spain) was appointed regional director in 2000 when Ian Hill became deputy director general. Nélida had been associate regional director in the Africa/Europe/Middle East office in Geneva since 1994. She studied at the University of Liège, Belgium (in French) and taught Spanish at the first IB diploma school in the Middle East – Iranzamin in Teheran, Iran – from 1971 to 1980. She then became head of Spanish and Directora Técnica at the International College Spain, Madrid, until she joined the IB.

In July 1992, while still in the Geneva office, Monica Flodman initiated the first five-day, annual (northern hemisphere) summer workshops in Szeged, Hungary, for teachers new to the IB Diploma Programme. It has become a tradition to hold them annually in Central/Eastern Europe or very close to that region (Vienna) and the number of participants has grown every year to more than 1830 in 2007 when they were held in Greece.

The IBAEM office operates in three official languages of the IB – English, French and Spanish – and, after North America, contains the largest number of state (public) IB schools. The major distribution of these schools is indicated in Table 3.

Country	public IB schools	total IB schools	% public
Sweden	32	34	94
Norway	15	21	71
Denmark	8	11	73

Finland	14	16	88
The Netherlands	11	15	73
United Kingdom	68	126	54
Spain	18	43	42
Germany	11	32	34
Poland	12	27	44

Table 3: Major distribution of public (state) IB schools in the Africa, Europe, Middle East region

There are 21 additional state schools in 17 countries, mostly in Central and Eastern Europe.

IB Asia-Pacific

Two part-time regional representatives were appointed in 1978 in this region. The last director of the IB Oxford Research Unit, Kevin Marjoribanks, Professor of Education at the University of Adelaide, was appointed in Australia. He continued in that role until 1982. After a nine-year period with no representative, Chris Brangwin, from the SCECGS Redlands School in Sydney, took on that role from 1991 and became full-time representative for the IB in Australasia from 1994. Greg Valentine replaced him in March 2001.

Eileen Davey of the International School, Makati, Philippines, was also appointed part-time (in 1978) to represent the IB in East Asia, followed by Peter Caleb of the same school in 1979 and 1980. Later, in 1980, John Goodban of the UWC in Singapore was appointed IB part-time regional representative for the region of South East Asia, including Australasia. In 1982 John organised the very first IB teacher training workshop in the region at the UWC of South East Asia in Singapore; it was a workshop on French B taken by Bernard Briquet.

In 1986 John worked 50% of his time as regional representative for what was now designated as Asia and 50% as deputy head of the UWC in Singapore. He became full-time regional director from 1991 for the Asia-Pacific region (another name change) until he retired in September 2002.

John Goodban developed a sub-regional representative structure to assist the Singapore headquarters. In 1988 he appointed Peter Jenks at the Kodaikanal International School, Tamil Nadu, as sub-regional representative for India. Peter remained in this post until 1994 when Mrs Farzana Dohadwalla in Mumbai took over as IB representative for South Asia, a post she still currently holds.

Shelley Gonzales was appointed sub-regional representative for South East Asia working from the Singapore office from 1994 until she left the IB organization in 2003. In 1996 Mrs Kyoko Bernard at the Yokohama International School and then at the Tamagawa University became sub-regional representative for Japan. Mrs Wang Hong in Beijing was appointed representative for China from 2000.

John's successor was Dr Helen Drennen (who had been the IB academic director in Cardiff from 1997) from November 2002 until May 2003 when she returned to take up a headship of Wesley College, Melbourne, Australia. Judith Guy was appointed regional director in August 2003. Judith's first teaching position was with Volunteer Service Abroad, in Western Samoa. Within education, Judith has had a variety of roles. These have included teaching middle and high school science, curriculum and IB programme coordination, university and college counselling, working as a Community Health Education Officer, and lecturing at the Cook Islands Teachers College. She has taught and worked as an administrator in national and international schools in New Zealand, the United Kingdom, the Netherlands, Western Samoa and the Cook Islands.

Since Chinese was introduced as an official language for the MYP in 1997, IBAP has had some staff who are native speakers of Chinese. In 2008 there are seven MYP schools teaching in Chinese and one PYP school – all in China; some of these are bilingual (Chinese/English). There are a handful of candidate schools in Hong Kong teaching bilingually (English/Chinese) MYP or PYP.

The region is vast. The fastest growth has been in Australia, which has 111 IB schools in January 2008 from two IB schools in 1982.

The regional office played a major role in responding to the tsunami disaster in December 2004, by employing a person full time to build a schools-to-schools assistance programme together with partnerships with international NGOs.

IB Latin America

Peter Stoyle, Head of the British Schools, Montevideo, Uruguay, was appointed Latin American representative in 1978. In 1979 Peter became director of studies at St George's College, Quilmes, Buenos Aires, Argentina, and continued as IB representative until 1982 when a regional office was officially established at the same location with Peter in charge. He was, at the same time, Latin American representative for the United World Colleges. The IB regional office moved to St Andrew's Scots School in northern Buenos Aires at the end of 1994. Peter remained regional director until his retirement in December 2000.

Peter Stoyle obtained a languages degree from Oxford and then did his diploma in education under Alec Peterson at the Department of Educational Studies in the late 1950s. His first teaching position was in Zimbabwe where he remained for four years. Ten years later, when Head of the British Schools Montevideo, Uruguay, Alec Peterson visited him and this led to that school being the first to offer the IB diploma course in Latin America.

The growth in Latin America and the vastness of that geographical area led to the appointment of Gabriel Green in Kingston, Jamaica, as Caribbean representative in 1983 and Leonardo Mayer in Mexico City as Mexican representative in 1984, in addition to the office in Buenos Aires. The Caribbean became the responsibility of IBNA from 1994. Mayer retired in 2001 and was not replaced.

The number of schools doubled in the four years since the office opened in 1982, and stood at 30 in 1986. By mid-1999 there were 130 authorised diploma schools in all major Latin American countries, with 17 authorised to teach the MYP and a similar number interested in the PYP. Growth was explosive in Argentina, from three to 38 diploma schools, making Buenos Aires, still today, the city with more IB schools than any other in the world.

In 2001, Marta Rodger was appointed regional director. An honours graduate from the Universidad de Buenos Aires with a degree in economics, and studies in sociology and education, she was involved in the implementation of the IB Diploma Programme in the Colegio de Todos los Santos, Buenos Aires. For ten years, as diploma coordinator, she became familiar with different aspects of the IB and was also able to gain experience as an IB teacher. Her incorporation to the IBLA regional office coincided with the launch of a new strategic plan, one of whose aims was to develop new systems in the offices to keep up with growth.

The increasing number of teacher-training workshops are organised in circuits where the workshop leaders fly to different national venues, mainly in IB schools, so that teachers do not have to fly long distances to these events. Originally these were rather leisurely in character, as there were few participants, but between October 1998 and February 1999 there were more than 1100 teachers who attended workshops. In 2004 there were more than 2250 teachers who attended workshops and more than 1150 who were trained by the IB in onsite school workshops. In 2007 the regional office trained 2931 teachers in their workshops and a further 1388 in onsite workshops making a total of 4319. The on site approach to workshops was implemented mainly for PYP but it also occurs for MYP and to a lesser extent for the Diploma Programme.

Recognition agreements with universities give an invaluable opportunity to meet with deans and academic administrators as they frequently are signed in an official signing ceremony. Agreements with universities have increased in the last few years, as a result of the larger number of diploma graduates attending their courses, and the collaborative work between the schools, the IB schools associations and the regional office.

The IB has aroused interest among some national educational authorities looking for models that could contribute to their national systems. In keeping with what Alec Peterson always saw as one of the functions of IB, the regional office has supported local initiatives to introduce the IB programmes in state schools. At present, two projects related to the implementation of the IB Diploma Programme are being developed in Ecuador and in Costa Rica. As a result, two state schools were authorized in Costa Rica in 2007 and authorization visits to state schools in Ecuador are planned for 2008.

Local associations of schools have sprung up since the early 1990s in Colombia, Venezuela, Argentina, Chile, Ecuador and Mexico, as they have done in other IB regions. In conjunction with the regional office, they organise a series of complementary activities such as teacher meetings, sub-regional conferences, and inter-school student events focusing on international theme debates, intensive ToK weekends, extended essay orientation, and inter-CAS meetings. In the last few years, a regional inter-CAS event has been taking place in different countries and students from different nationalities gather to participate in activities related to CAS.

Latin America is also the location of one of the original four schools offering the MYP as a pilot through the ISA as well as another whose director was part of the original thinking that led to the inauguration of MYP in the 1980s. These two pillar schools, St Catherine's Moorlands in Argentina and Santiago College in Chile, have both become IB World Schools implementing the three IB programmes.

The first MYP workshops took place in 1995 with the contribution of the pioneer schools at that time. During the last years, this programme showed an increased development in the region, especially with the programme flexibility that allows schools in Mexico not offering high school studies to benefit from the MYP.

Response to the PYP, for which the regional offices assumed the same responsibilities as for the other two programmes in 1997, saw the establishment of a team of five PYP consultants for the region. This group has been able to respond to requests for information seminars, and onsite workshops for schools due to enter their initial trial year. In 2003 a PYP manager was appointed to lead the increasing number of schools that are implementing this programme. In 2005 an associate PYP manager joined the office to contribute to the increased demand of this programme.

In the early days office facilities consisted mainly of an IBM typewriter, an old portable, and a telephone that could only dial direct within the country and to neighbouring Uruguay. International communication was through telexes relayed over the telephone to an agency in the city centre of Buenos Aires. In 2002 the IBLA office moved to a new site at a very modern office near the old premises. Bigger, with state-of-the-art technology, and a comfortable meeting room, it provided ample space for the increased number of staff who had been appointed to face the new challenges of the region. The office moved again in 2006 to larger premises. A more complex structure is now in place to provide academic support to the schools and their teachers, as well as functional support in the areas of finances, human resources, administration, and conferences and workshops.

In spite of the economic crises that the region has suffered in the last 15 years, in particular Argentina from 2002, IB schools have strived to meet annual subscription costs to remain part of the IB World School network. Today, IB schools are models for others in Latin America seeking quality educational opportunities for children.

Note

1. As at 2010, these details can be updated as follows:

    2005-2007: Delia Pompa, president
    2007-2008: Carl Amrhein, president

    The IBNA board ceased to exist in October 2008.

2. This organisation changed its name in 2003 to the *Société des établissements du baccalauréat international du Québec* (Society of international baccalaureate schools of Quebec).

References

Avanzini, G., et al (1979): *The International Bureau of Education in the Service of Educational Development.* UNESCO, Paris.

Blackburn, R., (1988): *A D C Peterson, OBE, DEd (Hon), 1908-1988: a tribute.* Geneva: IBO.

Boeke, K., (1948): Letter to the Assistant Director General for UNESCO. Dated 5th August 1948. Paris: UNESCO archives.

Bonner, R., (1990): Hatching the international baccalaureate, in *Contact (the journal of the IB schools),* No 3, October, pp40-41.

Bonner, R., (1991): Teacher at the International School of Geneva 1955-63; IBO executive secretary 1965-80. Interview in Geneva 10th December 1991.

Carus, B., (1992): Trustee of the Hegeler Institute; chairman of Open Court Publishing House; founding member of IB North America; member of IBO Council of Foundation 1973-94. Interview in Geneva 1st December 1992.

CAS (1989): *CAS Activities: Guidelines for IBO Schools.* IBO. Geneva.

Cole-Baker, D., (ed) (1970): *An International Primary School Curriculum ISA.* International Schools Association. Geneva.

Cole-Baker, D., (1989): Personal correspondence with the author. 16th April 1989. New Zealand.

Cole-Baker, D., (1990): The international baccalaureate why and how: a personal recollection, in *Contact (the journal of the international baccalaureate schools),* No3, October, pp37-39.

Cole-Baker, D., (1992): Personal correspondence with the author. 24th March 1992. New Zealand.

Collège Cévénol (1946): *Handbook.* November. Chambon-sur-Lignon, France.

Conference of Principals of International Schools (1949): Minutes of the first meeting held at UNESCO house on the 31st March and 1st April 1949. Paris: UNESCO archives.

Conference of Principals of International Schools and Schools Specially Interested in Developing International Understanding (1951): Report of the Second Meeting. Paris: UNESCO archives.

Course for Teachers Interested in International Education: Final Report (1950): International School of Geneva 23 July-19 August 1950. Paris: UNESCO archives.

Decorvet, P., (1981): La Préparation au Baccalauréat International à l'Ecole Internationale de Genève, in *Conférence Suisse des Directeurs Cantonaux de l'Instruction Publique: Bulletin d'Information,* No 26, Mai 1981, pp45-56.

Dickson, A., (1984): Letter to Robert Blackburn. 22 June. IB archives. Geneva.

Ecole Internationale de Genève: 50e Anniversaire 1924-1974 (1974): Genève.

Ecole Européenne: Informations Générales (1991): Bruxelles.

Egger, E., (1981): L'intérêt du Baccalauréat International pour la Suisse, in *Conférence Suisse des Directeurs Cantonaux de l'Instruction Publique: Bulletin d'Information,* No 26, Mai 1981, pp8-9.

Ferrière, A., (1925): Letter concerning a *Maturité Internationale.* Dated 24 January 1925. From the archives of the International School of Geneva.

Ficheux, R., et al (1949): Some Suggestions on the Teaching of Geography, in *Towards World Understanding* series, No 7. Paris, UNESCO.

First Conference of Teachers of Social Studies in International Schools: Report. (1962): International School of Geneva. 26 August-1st September 1962.

Ford Foundation Annual Report (1966): New York.

Fox, E., (1985): International schools and the IB, in *Harvard Educational Review*, Vol 55, No 1, February, pp53-68.

Gathier, P., (1992): Director general of secondary education 1966-72 then director general of education 1972-86, the Netherlands; President of the IBO Council of Foundation 1984-1990. Interview in Geneva. 2nd December 1992.

Gellar, C., (1991): Head, International School of Copenhagen 1968-85; director, Brussels' English Primary Schools since 1985. Interview in Birmingham 17th November 1991.

Goormaghtigh, J., (1991): Director, European office of the Carnegie Endowment for international peace until 1979; president of the IBO Council of Foundation 1967-80; Secretary-General, European Science Foundation 1979-87. Interview in Geneva 13th November 1991.

Hameline, D., (1985-86): Adolphe Ferrière 1879-1960, in Zaghloul, M., (ed), *Thinkers on Education*, Vol 1. Paris: UNESCO. 1985-86, pp373-401.

Hampton, A., (1976): Sense and Sensibility in an International Context, in *Comparative Education*, Vol 12, No 3, October, pp267-74

Hanson, H., (1971): The international baccalaureate, in *International Education and Cultural Exchange*, Vol 7, No 1, Summer, pp10-14.

Hanson, H., (1992): Director, Advanced Placement Programme, College Entrance Examination Board, US 1965-99. Interview at Séléstat (near Strasbourg), France 17th October 1992.

Hayden, M., Richards, P., Thompson, J., (1995): Validity and reliability issues in International Baccalaureate examinations, in T. Kellaghan (ed), *Admission to Higher Education: Issues and Practice*. pp131-41. Princeton: International Association of Educational Assessment.

Hayot, P., (1984): *The IB: a study of the evolution of international education in France since 1976*. PhD thesis. University of Michigan, USA.

Hill, C., (1953): Suggestions on the Teaching of History, in *Towards World Understanding* series, No 9. Paris, UNESCO.

Hill, I., (1994): *The international baccalaureate: policy process in education*. PhD thesis. University of Tasmania, Australia.

HSC (1981): Heads Standing Conference, New York. 1981. IB archives. Geneva.

IB (1964): Report of USA visit by R Leach to introduce ISES. 1-15 April 1964. IB archives, Geneva.

IB (1967): Sèvres conference report: joint sessions of commissions A and B. 1967. IB archives, Geneva.

IB (1968): *IBO Semi Annual Bulletin,* 1968, No 1. IB archives, Geneva.

IB (1969): *IBO Director-General's annual report 1969-70*. IB archives, Geneva.

IB (1969a): *IBO Semi Annual Bulletin*, 1969, No 3. IB archives, Geneva.

IB (1969b): *IBO Semi Annual Bulletin*, 1969, No 2. IB archives, Geneva.

IB (1970): *General Guide to the International Baccalaureate*. 1970. IB Office, Geneva.

IB (1970a): *IBO Semi Annual Bulletin*, 1970, No 4. IB archives, Geneva.

IB (1970b): *IBO Semi Annual Bulletin*, 1970, No 5. IB archives, Geneva.

IB (1970c): *Declaration of Trust*. IB archives, Geneva.

IB (1971a): *IBO Semi Annual Bulletin*, 1971, No 6. IB archives, Geneva.

IB (1971b): *IBO Semi Annual Bulletin*, 1971, No 7. IB archives, Geneva.

IB (1972): *General Guide to the International Baccalaureate*. 1972. IB Office, Geneva.

IB (1972a): *IBO Annual Bulletin*, No 8, 1972. IB archives, Geneva.

IB (1973): *IBO Annual Bulletin*, No 9, 1973. IB archives, Geneva.

IB (1973a): *IBO Director General's Annual Report 1973-74*. IB archives, Geneva.

IB (1974): *Sevres IB Evaluation Conference Report*. 22-26 April 1974. IB archives, Geneva.

IB (1974a): *IBO Annual Bulletin*, No 10, 1974. IB archives, Geneva.

IB (1975): *IBO Annual Bulletin*, No 11, 1975. IB archives, Geneva.

IB (1975a): *IBO Director General's Annual Report 1975-76*. IB archives, Geneva.

IB (1976): *IBO Annual Bulletin*, No 12, 1976. IB archives, Geneva.

IB (1977): *General Guide to the International Baccalaureate*. 1977. IB Office, Geneva.

IB (1977a): *IBO Annual Bulletin*, No 13, 1977. IB archives, Geneva.

IB (1978): *IBO Annual Bulletin*, No 14, 1978. IB archives, Geneva.

IB (1978a): *Inter-governmental Conference Report*. Second conference, London. 15-16 February 1978. IB archives, Geneva.

IB (1979): *IBO Annual Bulletin*, No 15, 1979. IB archives, Geneva.

IB (1980): General Guide to the International Baccalaureate. 1980. IB Office, Geneva.

IB (1980a): *IBO Annual Bulletin*, No 16, 1980. IB archives, Geneva.

IB (1981): *IBO Annual Bulletin*, No 17, 1981. IB archives, Geneva.

IB (1981a): *Inter-governmental Conference Report*: Third conference, Brussels. 3-5 February 1981. IB Archives, Geneva.

IB (1982): *IBO Annual Bulletin*, No 18, 1982. IB archives, Geneva.

IB (1983): *IBO Annual Bulletin*, No 19, 1983. IB archives, Geneva.

IB (1984): *IBO Annual Bulletin*, No 20, 1984. IB archives, Geneva.

IB (1985): *General Guide to the International Baccalaureate*. 1985. IB Office, Geneva.

IB (1985a): *IBO Annual Bulletin*, No 21, 1985. IB archives, Geneva.

IB (1985): *IBO Annual Bulletin*, No 22, 1986. IB archives, Geneva.

IB (1987): *IBO Annual Bulletin*, No 23, 1987. IB archives, Geneva.

IB (1989): *IBO Annual Bulletin*, No 25, 1989. IB archives, Geneva.

IB (1990): IB council of foundation, 23rd meeting minutes. IB archives, Geneva.

IB (1991): Minutes of the 70th meeting of the executive committee. 11 & 14 November 1991. IB archives, Geneva.

IB (1992): *The Complete Guide to Extended Essays*. 1992. IBO. Geneva.

IB (2001): *Creativity, Action, Service*. 2001. IBO. Geneva.

International School of Geneva Student-Parent Handbook (1924): Geneva.

International School of Geneva, Board Minutes 4 June (1962): [official title in French: *Procès verbal de la séance du conseil de direction de l'Association de l'Ecole Internationale de Genève*]

International School of Geneva, Board Minutes. 9 March (1965): [official title in French: *Procès verbal de la séance du conseil de direction de l'Association de l'Ecole Internationale de Genève*]

ISA (1953): *International Schools Association. Minutes of Annual Assemblies or Conferences from 1953*. IB Organisation archives, Geneva.

ISA (1955): *Fourth Assembly Minutes*. IBO archives. Geneva.

ISA (1956): *International Schools Association Fifth Assembly Minutes*. IB Organisation, Geneva.

ISA (1957): *International Schools Association Sixth Assembly Minutes*. IB Organisation, Geneva.

ISA (1959): *International Schools Association Eighth Assembly Minutes*. IB Organisation, Geneva.

ISA (1960): *International Schools Association Ninth Assembly Minutes*. IB Organisation, Geneva.

ISA (1961): *International Schools Association Tenth Assembly Minutes*. IB Organisation, Geneva.

ISA (1962): *International Schools Association Eleventh Assembly Minutes*. IB Organisation, Geneva.

ISA (1962a): Research Project Submitted to the Twentieth Century Fund by ISA. IBO archives. Geneva.

ISA (1964): *International Schools Association Minutes of the Thirteenth General Assembly*. IB archives. Geneva

ISA (1968): *International Schools Association Seventeenth Assembly Minutes*. IB Organisation, Geneva.

ISA (1968a): Annual conference report. IB Organisation, Geneva.

ISA (1968b): Report on the International Baccalaureate August 1967 to July 1968. IBO archives. Geneva.

ISA (1969): Report on the International Baccalaureate August 1968 to July 1969. IBO archives. Geneva.

ISES (1964): International Schools Examination Syndicate Day Report, May 1964. IB archives, Geneva

ISES (1964a): International Schools Examination Syndicate Report (February 1964). IB archives. Geneva.

International Schools Liaison Committee Minutes, 20 November 1951 & 6 December 1952. Paris: UNESCO archives

Knight, M., (1992): Personal correspondence with the author. 31st March 1992. Geneva.

Knight, M., (1999): *Ecolint: a portrait of the International School of Geneva 1924-1999*. Geneva: International School of Geneva.

Knight, M., and Leach, R., (1964): International secondary schools, in Bereday, G., and Lauwerys, J., (eds), *Education and international life*. London: Evans Brothers. pp443-457.

Leach, R., (1962): Report of consultant on his year's work: 1961-62, ISA document: Geneva

Leach, R., (1969a): *International schools and their role in the field of international education*. New York: Pergamon Press.

Leach, R., (1969b): Origins and development of the IB, in *Independent School Bulletin* 28 (3) February, pp80-82.

Leach, R., (1991): Teacher and head of history at the International School of Geneva 1951-81; ISA consultant 1961-62. Interview in Geneva 13th December 1991.

Leach, R., (1991a): Personal correspondence with Dr Roger Peel, director general of the IB Organization, 21st November 1991, Geneva

Maclehose, A., (1971): *The International Baccalaureate*. MEd thesis, University of Wales, UK.

Malinowski, H., and Zorn, V., (1973): *The United Nations International School: its history and development*. UNIS, New York.

Maurette, M., (1948): *Techniques d'éducation pour la paix: existent-ils? (Réponse à une enquête de l'UNESCO)*. Monograph. International School of Geneva.

Mayer, M., (1968): *Diploma: international schools and university entrance*. New York: Twentieth Century Fund.